A Fly-Switch from the Sultan

FOR SUSAN

A Fly-Switch
from the Sultan

DARRELL BATES

Illustrated by
MARGERY GILL

RUPERT HART-DAVIS
SOHO SQUARE LONDON
1961

PRINTED IN GREAT BRITAIN BY
WESTERN PRINTING SERVICES LTD, BRISTOL

Contents

Contents

"My First Elephant" is reprinted by permission of *Punch*. Several of the other chapters were originally broadcast by the B.B.C. in an abridged form.

CHAPTER ONE

The Beginning

I was on a farm in Suffolk, making hay, when it arrived. It was a large and imposing-looking envelope and the postman, who liked to know what was going on, clearly had no intention of leaving until he had found out in a general way what was inside it.

It said that I had been selected as a cadet of the Colonial Administrative Service in Tanganyika. Neither the postman nor I knew exactly where Tanganyika was, but the girl who did the milking, and was rather a know-all, said it was sure to be somewhere in Africa. There was a catch in it, of course: subject, they said all this was, to your passing a medical test. A week later I went up for this medical thing. I thought it

7

would create a good impression if I arrived bursting with health and vigour so I hired a bicycle and rode up to London. It was a hot summer, and by the time I arrived at the Colonial Office I looked like the pictures one saw of West African gin-traders in the last stages of malaria.

Anyway, they passed me. They didn't even look at my leg muscles. I might just as well have gone up on the 8.35.

The pay was three hundred and fifty pounds a year. It seemed a lot of money in 1935.

First of all there was another year at Oxford. The programme was carefully designed to produce a gang of semi-skilled Poo-Bahs. It ranged from various Oriental and African languages to explosives. In between were things like surveying (in the Parks), map-reading (mainly in the Lamb and Flag) and first-aid (mainly in the nurses' hostel at the Radcliffe Infirmary). It was a wonderful year.

Among other things I bought a car. It was a 1924 Austin Twelve and it cost five pounds. A year later, the day before we sailed for Africa, I drove it into the tradesman's entrance at Fulham Palace and left it there. I had given it to a friend of mine whose uncle was a bishop. A year after that, when he too came out to Tanganyika, he sent me a cheque for three pounds, which is what the scrap merchant had given him.

We spent the last month or so on problems of equipment. My mother had died when I was a child and my father at the time was wandering in a scholarly fashion in Mexico, so I had to do most of this myself. But although at twenty-two one doesn't of course need any help with anything, I did make one or two mistakes.

Pith helmets, for instance. Tropical outfitters had a wonderful and persuasive range of these and I bought several. A Bombay Bowler one was called, and there was another with a flap at the back like the thing female tortoises wear to deter predatory males. But in the end I gave them all away to chiefs and houseboys and bought a Panama.

Cholera-belts and spine-pads were other mistakes. There was a shiny-faced colonel who had been in India in the nineties and he gave us a series of hair-raising lectures on Tropical Hygiene. "The filthy feet of defecating flies" was a pet phrase of his. Anyway, he was very keen on cholera-belts (to prevent a chill on the tummy in the treacherous early hours) and spine-pads (to keep the murderous tropical sun from the back of the neck). I bought a spine-pad, and a girl I knew knitted me one of the other things. Eventually, unworn, they found their way to a sale of work where they fetched ninepence the pair.

There were other mistakes as well. But even the parents slipped up sometimes. I know of one mother who sent her son to Africa with a crateful of lavatory-paper. She had worked out the amount needed, with a little extra for visitors and a bonus in case he got married. She used a slide-rule, or so I was told.

The odds and ends of stories in this book are an attempt to show roughly what we did and what sort of lives we led when we arrived in Africa. They are very much out of date now. Both the country and the people have changed a lot in the last fifteen years or so; and I am quite sure that, whatever some people may say or wish to believe, they have changed for the better. If I have painted a picture of an unsophisticated people it is not in order to point any finger of scorn. It is rather to emphasize what tremendous changes and advances have taken place, and to pay my small but very sincere tribute both to the African peoples who have achieved them and to the small band of Administrative Officers of the Colonial Service whose monument these achievements are.

CHAPTER TWO

First Footsteps

THE LORRY was over an hour late. For this hour I sat, with apprehension for company, among my boxes and bags.

The largest of them was the bath. A great oval of smooth brown enamel, it sat there waiting patiently for all the battering and chipping that Africa was to do to it. There were black tin boxes with my name on them in shining white letters. There were camp-beds and tables and chairs new and unused like myself. Further off the cook and the houseboy, even newer acquisitions, were sitting among the pots and pans and lamps. They talked together in quiet fluid voices.

I couldn't follow what they were saying, although they were

talking in a language which on paper I already knew. But here, waiting under the climbing sun and the coconut trees, the words grooved into one another more smoothly and more quickly than I could follow. When I tried to use them myself they stuck in my throat and, when hesitantly they emerged, they were pale and false shadows of the true.

When at last the lorry arrived I hadn't the confidence of words or manner to ask why it was late. But I needn't have bothered. The driver leant over the metal door and grinned with gappy teeth.

"This lorry," he explained. "Much trouble."

This was one word I already knew by heart.

For the first few miles out of the town the road was a road. The tarmac quickly gave way to metal, but there were stone hedges and culverts, and houses and gardens along the side to define it before these too were left behind. For the rest of the way it was a marginless, dusty, eroded track.

The lorry ploughed its furrows in the dust and left a thick red cloud behind it. When we slowed down to breast a hill or to negotiate a gully the cloud would catch up and envelop us. By the time the lorry boiled for the first time, we were all covered in dust from head to foot. I looked at my watch. It was a quarter-past ten. We had done less than twenty miles in an hour and a half. At this rate, I thought, we wouldn't get in until dusk.

It was several hours and a few dozen miles on that the driver tapped me on the arm. I had been dozing in the heat and the dust.

"Look!" he said. "Look!"

Since we had left the town we had seen very little on the road. I had expected files of women with pots on their heads and of men half-naked and armed with spears, and in between, of course, elephant and lion and zebra and snakes. But there had been nothing. Just miles and miles of empty untenanted bush.

At first I couldn't see a thing. The driver had slowed down and the dust had caught up and swallowed us. And then I saw him.

It was a leopard. He stood on the side of the road, alone and aloof and confident of his claws and his speed. When we got closer he turned and with one unhurried liquid movement he disappeared into the bush. My heart was hammering against my ribs. If I close my eyes now I can still see him, and remember the impact on my English mind of this first truly wild and savage thing. It was years before I saw another leopard.

That was all we saw. Every time we came to a hill or a patch of sand the engine would boil. Waiting for it to cool off, or sitting in the lorry while it heated up again, I had plenty of time to think.

A month ago I had been driving along Cotswold lanes on my way to London. I knew what lay round each corner in front of me. When I stopped there was a pub with cool brown ale and a barmaid with a country flush in her cheeks. When I reached London there were houses and people that I had visited before. Their speech and their silences were familiar to me. It all seemed a long way away.

"Rain, Bwana."

I had had my eyes shut. For a moment the unfamiliar word and the unfamiliar title eluded me. Then I opened my eyes and looked at the dark clouds and the harsh orange light in the sky. A few moments later the first heavy drops of rain chattered against the windscreen like hail.

We stuck the first time in a slight hollow. The red dust had turned quickly to a greasy mud. The wheels of the lorry slipped off the crown of the road and then settled deep in the soft mire at the side. When the wheel had been raised on the thick heavy length of the jack, brushwood and coconut fronds were trampled in underneath it. In the end the wheel caught and slithered on to the road. The engine had boiled again and it was some time before we could start. Ten minutes later we stuck again.

By the time we got to the river the sun was settling down for the night behind the trees. There was a drift of stone and branches across the river. The muddied water poured across it like a stream of liquid chocolate. The driver cut the engine and got out. He walked a few paces across the causeway lifting his white waistcloth above his knees. The water swirled round his brown legs.

When he came back he shook his head. We sat in the lorry waiting for the rain to stop. I gave him a cigarette.

"How long?" I asked.

He shrugged.

"Only God knows. Four hours. Or five. Or six." His sense of time was easy and elastic.

"Once a lorry tried to cross here when the river was running like this." When he spoke slowly, using simple words, I could follow him. "They found it twenty miles away."

I thought that his sense of distance was probably elastic as well. But he had made his point.

By the time the rain had stopped it was quite dark. In the path of the headlamps they put up my camp-bed under the thick green umbrella of a mango tree. The cook had conjured a fire from sticks and coconut husks and paraffin and had made some tea. I drank it from a large tin mug. It was hot and sweet and strong. No brew had ever tasted better.

I sat on the camp-bed listening to the noise of the cicadas— a harsh persistent burr like the engaged sound of a telephone.

In the distance there was a sudden strange unearthly cry of suffering and sadness. I didn't know what it was, and inside me there grew unease and a small fear. In the end I went across to the second mango tree where the driver and the others were crouched round a smouldering fire. I asked what it was.

"Fisi," they said. "It is nothing."

The houseboy, whose name was Ali, and who came from Nyasaland, got up and walked back with me.

He picked up the lamp and put it carefully at the foot of the bed. It would, he explained, keep the lions away. Then, having made sure I was looking, he picked it up again and put it at the other end by the pillow.

"That is better," he said.

I wondered what all this was leading to. He came to the point by a devious route.

"This place we are going to. It is far from the town. It is lonely."

"Yes," I said. What else could I say?

"I am your servant. For three days I have worked for you. I will work for you faithfully until I die."

There was much that I couldn't follow but I think this was the gist of it.

"I have recently taken a wife. She is a good wife but," he added with a touch of drama, "she was very expensive. A hundred shillings I must pay her father."

Five pounds. It was certainly a lot of money.

"So far I have paid twenty-three shillings."

By now I could see the end of this particular road quite clearly.

There was a longish pause and then, with commendable subtlety, he arranged the mosquito-net over my bed and said good night.

When he had gone I got the dictionary out of my bag. *Fisi* was the word for a hyena. I laughed at my fears. But I had an uncanny feeling that both the hyena and Ali had won the first round on points.

It rained again the next day and it was nearly five in the evening when the driver turned his head and said,

"There. That is the place."

But there was not very much to see. Beyond a fringe of bush along the road there were patches of cultivation. There were a few scattered huts of coconut leaves plaited and sewn with twine. Some children naked and brown and solemn were playing in the dust. We turned a corner and between the coconut trees I could see the sea winking like metal in the glare. Suddenly there was a long white building turreted like a *Beau Geste* fort. Above it a Union Jack hung a little torn, and limp and listless. But it still somehow held a hint of authority and calm.

I took a deep breath. This after all was what I had travelled twenty-odd years and six thousand miles to do.

A flight of steps led from the dusty road to the white turreted building. At the top of them a long, angular figure in crumpled white trousers and white shirt was waiting. His face was long and lean and grey. It was all nose and Adam's apple.

The District Commissioner was a character, people had said. He was the younger son of an Earl, but that, it seemed, must have been a long time and a long distance ago. His digestion was a trouble to him, and the moth seemed to have got into his hair and his clothes. With a thin barking voice and harsh eccentricities he sought to conceal a gentle nature and a kindly heart. He smiled a toothy smile when I said who I was.

"Ah yes," he said. He looked at the lorry and the new tin boxes covered with mud and dust, and then he looked at me.

"I hadn't expected you so soon."

I didn't know what to say. He had a large fly-switch made from a mane of a lion in his thin bony hands and he twitched it to brush the flies off his face.

"Well, I'm off for my evening walk," he said.

Then without another word he went down the steps, and I watched as the tall white figure disappeared along the track that led through the coconut trees down to the sea. The fly-switch trailed behind him like a ceremonial goat—hairy and slightly smelly—and though I did not know it at the time it was in fact a sort of badge of office.

CHAPTER THREE

Bagamoyo

M<small>Y FIRST</small> year in Africa was spent in this place. It was called Bagamoyo. Although it had had, in its time, a wicked past compounded in more or less equal parts of ivory and slaves and the sort of urban vices which are now becoming fashionable in S.W.3, it was, when I was there, a quiet and quite unimportant little town. It had an administrative area attached to it about the size of three English counties, and we were supposed to cherish and chastise this area, and all that was in it, like an omnibus Rural District Council.

Tanganyika was run on a shoestring in those days, in the aftermath of the economic depression of the early thirties, and there were only the two of us. The District Commissioner, who was a man of about fifty, had years of Africa behind, and to some extent inside, him. He was more or less king. Louis XIV may have thought that *l'état c'est moi*; but even Richelieu, who like a good Chief of Staff probably invented the phrase to keep the King happy while he himself held the reins, would I think have been surprised at the way this seed flowered in the fields of District Commissioners in the years between the wars in Africa. More often than not it was benevolent despotism. "You are my father and my mother," they used to say to us, and not all of them were just sycophants. But it was despotism all the same.

The other one was me. I was twenty-two and very new. The isolation and the quietness and the unimportance of Bagamoyo were a great blessing in two ways. The absence of European visitors made it easier for me to concentrate on learning the essential elements of my job. Firstly the language, that was one's bridge to the people on the other bank, and then, at first hesitantly and then completely absorbed, the discovery of the nature and the quality of the people who lived there.

The other advantage was that I could wear off a certain amount of my greenness and make some of my worst mistakes in comparative obscurity. This was a great help.

Although there were two of us we weren't very often or very long in the same place at the same time. Not only was the District large in size but communications were rather sketchy, so that the remoter parts were attached by tenuous administrative threads which had been knotted *ad hoc* in so many places that they looked like a drawing by Heath Robinson and needed constant repair.

The result was that one of us was out visiting and travelling most of the time. My District Commissioner had two particular hates which, in their own way, were great assets. He hated Christmas and he hated what he used to call mechanical contrivances.

So he always went on safari at Christmas, and he always travelled on foot.

The first meant that I could safely invite some friends of mine from Dar-es-Salaam to share a goose, some tinned Christmas pudding and four bottles of whisky. I also had a Christmas-tree, of local origin, and we hung the presents on the thorns. It was a very good party, as it happened, except that the knob-nosed goose which I shot as it flighted over the river was taken by a crocodile when it hit the water so we had roast goat instead.

His other hate led me, perforce, to realize that if you want to know what really goes on in your District and what the people are really like, the thing to do is to walk.

I was a bachelor then. Generally speaking, wives and walking don't go together.

"Yes," people would say when later I was back in England on leave, "but what do you actually do?"

Although I had spent two and a half years doing it, it was a question that I always found difficult to answer. Part of the trouble was that one did so many things, and so few of them somehow seemed to have any ready English counterpart. In backwater Districts where there was only a District Commissioner and, with luck, an Assistant, there were no magistrates (Inner Temple and all that), no police officers, no agricultural or forestry or veterinary experts, no proper builders or road-menders. So we did the lot. One spent a lot of time in court and, although in practice we mostly just used our common sense to find a fair answer, we often had to thumb through Archbold or somebody on torts afterwards to see if it also agreed with the law. People in England, particularly judges, often looked surprised when they heard that as well as being a magistrate I ran the police detachment, and the prison as well. In between times we read books on soil erosion and dipping of cattle and ring-barking and so were able to pass on the benefits of Western civilization to our flock. We also mended and, if need be, built roads and hospitals and houses and schools, and one or two other things as well. I once even ran a brothel, but that was in Abyssinia during the war when I was in the Army.

This first year or so was a sort of apprenticeship. You were called a cadet and at the end of it, if you were lucky, you were confirmed. Instead of a catechism there were exams in law and in the language. It was lonely and sometimes the weeks and the months seemed very long, but it was always interesting and often it was fun.

CHAPTER FOUR

First Safari

I HAD decided in the end to walk at the rear of the column This was my first safari and I was keen to do the right thing I could, I suppose, have asked the District Commissioner but he was apt to be caustic before breakfast, and would probably have said it didn't matter a damn where you walked. "If you had any sense," he might have added, "you would walk in the opposite direction."

As the long file of porters strung out in front of me along the track in the long wiry grass I could hardly believe my eyes. This, at any rate, was just like Sanders of the River. They were singing, and, although this was East and not West Africa, the high-pitched solo and the deep guttural chorus seemed to come straight from Edgar Wallace.

The porters, it is true, were not like the strapping naked savages I had seen in the film. They were quiet, thin-legged men with yards of cloth round their waists and coloured scarves over their shoulders. They smiled shyly when one spoke to them, and they rarely laughed. They had Mohammedan names like Ali and Hassan and Hamisi. They were very nice people.

We had been walking for about an hour when the first excited shouts began.

"Mnyama! Mnyama!"

It started a long way ahead as a thin echo. Quickly it spread down the line of porters until it seemed to come from inside my own excited, bursting chest. This, I knew it, was the Moment of Truth.

"An animal! wild game!" That was the call. Quickly I seized my rifle from the cook, who was carrying it nonchalantly together with the saucepan he had forgotten to pack with the kitchen stores. I made my way ahead to shield my defenceless porters. I should have been at the head of the column after all, I thought, as I ran past the bath and the camp-chairs and the boxes of tinned beef. I pictured a lion, a wounded buffalo or an angry boar, and wondered vaguely where on earth to aim for.

When I reached the head of the column my worst fears seemed to be confirmed: along the track boxes and loads lay scattered and abandoned in the grass. To the left were some of the porters shouting and running wildly and waving their arms.

It did look though, I must confess, as if they were running after and not away from whatever it was. I went towards them but with a less certain stride.

"What is it?" I asked.

"There! Look!" The porter was a small spindly man but his eyes were shining.

I looked. I followed his pointing finger, and there it was. It looked very like an English rabbit at first glance, but it was a hare, a wild African hare.

After that I walked at the head of the column. I was glad when we reached the sea and our path lay along the sand. Not even the crabs, though edible, could evoke those ear-splitting compelling cries of hunt and chase.

We camped by a village on the shore. The headman called himself a Shirazi—an Oriental with origins that went back hundreds of years to the Persian Gulf. His ancestors came as exiled, adventuring men, and stayed to marry and rule and grow coconuts and decline. He had a long bearded face and his speech and his manners were finely grained. When he recited his ancestry, which he did at length, it sounded like the Old Testament.

I lay on my bed that night under the stars and watched the Southern Cross pivot its way across the sky. The sea lapped quietly in the sand, and the porters snored scratchily round the fire.

There were mangrove swamps farther up the coast, and although my destination was another place on the sea, the path went inland from the village. In the long grass we saw some buffalo and I shot one to provide meat for the porters. Normally buffalo are cunning and dangerous, but these were small and slow and timorous. The reason, I was told by the headman, who accompanied us to the end of his land, was that his forebears used to keep cattle. But disease had reduced the herds and the abolition of slavery by the misguided European had reduced the herdsmen until the cows had become errant and were covered by the wild buffalo from the forest.

The next night we camped by a river. It was a small river and there were no hippo, but there were crocodile basking arrogantly on the sandbanks. We set the camp in the cool fresh shade of some banana trees. A few days before some elephant had been attracted by these trees and had camped there as well. There were not many bananas left.

It was difficult to find level ground for chairs and tables and beds as it was pitted with marks like enormous soup-plates. I thought everyone was very stupid to choose a place like this to camp in, but, sensing the reason for my irritation, they assured me that at this time of the year elephant were on the move and wouldn't come back to finish off the bananas.

"Already," they said, "they are miles and miles away over there."

I knew better, of course, and kept a careful watch. But there was not even a stray pussy cat to disturb our sleep.

We reached the town the following evening. It wasn't really a town but it was marked in large letters on the map. The map had been printed thirty years before, and the reason for the large print was that a hundred years earlier it had been a flourishing port for ivory and slaves. It had gone steadily downhill, and by now it was like a roué looking over his shoulder at the past before he tripped, an exhausted ruin, into his grave. The houses in the main street were crumbling and the dogs and the children slept on the dusty paths un-disturbed.

Among other mundane things like collecting tax, and settling disputes and repairing the drains I had one very delicate thing to do in this place.

I left it until the end.

On the last day I called the headman and told him to arrange a meeting. When I arrived there were about sixty females of assorted shades and shapes. Most of the people of the coast were Muslims and for conventional modesty the women wore veils and black shrouds to hide the brightly patterned cloth that was wound tightly round their forms. The veils hid all but the eyes, or a corner of the black shroud was held across the face to conceal or reveal as the owner wished. They were assembled in the court-house. It had a low stone wall and a roof, thatched with the palms of coconut. It was open at the sides, and a few children had collected outside to listen and yawn and spit. Most of the young men had left the sinking ship to seek their fortunes elsewhere. It was hot, and all the old men were asleep. Or perhaps they had sensed that this was not for them.

I had not addressed a female gathering like this before. I had once given a lecture at a Women's Institute in Gloucestershire, but the subject had been much less complicated and the eyes that faced me now with unabashed expectancy were also a good deal less demure.

"Some time ago," I began, "a man was brought into the hospital in the big town. He was carried on a stretcher because he could not walk. He was very ill and near to death."

A whisper ran through the crowd.

"He means old Sheikh Abdulla."

The sense of expectancy increased, and above the veils the eyes became even less demure.

"He came from this village," I went on. I used a derogatory expression of excessive smallness to underline my disapproval. Sadly, it went unnoticed.

"Now he has nearly recovered from his injury and his indignity, and soon he will return to his house. But," and here I made what I hoped was a dramatic pause, "but save for the grace of God he would be dead."

A hushed murmur seeped through the gathering.

"Al hamdu illahi? Thanks be to God!" they said.

The pious atmosphere was somewhat spoiled by what sounded ominously like a giggle from the back of the crowd. I ignored it.

"He had been assaulted," I went on. "He had been shamefully assaulted. And what makes it worse was that he was assaulted in the privacy of his home by his wife."

I paused once more.

"By his own wife. And that no more than a girl."

I was going to add "young enough to be his daughter" but on second thoughts I thought that would be better left unsaid. Sheikh Abdulla was a long way past his prime and I didn't want the effect to be spoilt by any unseemly gust of laughter.

"If he had died," I went on again, "his wife would have been tried for murder." I let the awful word sink in. "She might have been hanged."

I had the crowd quiet now. They seemed at last to be taking the thing seriously. But I wasn't quite sure how to go on.

"The District Commissioner has instructed me to warn you, O women and girls of this town . . ." I knew I was beginning to sound a bit pompous. I would very much have liked a drink, ". . . to warn you of the shamefulness, of the iniquity, of the dangers of assaulting your husbands in that way."

I let this sink in, and then came the question. It was a difficult question in any case. What made it worse was that the questioner, and indeed all the women there, clearly knew what the answer was.

"In what way exactly," said the voice, "was he assaulted?"

Early next morning I set off again with my porters. I left

earlier than was usual. I hoped that everyone would be asleep. But as we passed in single file through the town I knew that behind every shutter and every door the women were watching. I hoped I would never have to visit that place again. And indeed I never did.

CHAPTER FIVE

Shotgun Saturday

I ALWAYS had a curry lunch on Saturdays. After lacing the lining of my stomach with cold beer I would fill it up with popadums and chillies and excesses of other heating materials. The result was a coma from which I would emerge at about five o'clock, dry-mouthed and bad-tempered. But on balance it was worth it.

On this particular Saturday I was about halfway on the road to coma when Ali came in. Both his cap and his expression had clearly been put on in a hurry.

"What is it?" I asked in my not-to-be-disturbed voice.

"Trouble." Ali who came from a long way up-country had a laconic sense of drama.

"What sort of trouble?"

"Bad trouble."

He turned then, and soon afterwards I heard him rummaging about in my bedroom. When he came back he had something under his arm. He put it down carefully on a chair and opened the lid.

The end of Act One, I thought.

The barrel of the shotgun was smooth and gleaming and unused. At the ends the two dark, empty eyes looked at me with a hollow smile.

"All this cleaning and polishing," they seemed to say. "Now let's see if you can put it to any good purpose."

"What is the trouble?" I asked again.

"It is in the kitchen," Ali replied. He opened the packet and put the No. 3 cartridges on the table.

"What is in the kitchen, Ali?" I knew I must get this settled before the coma set in. I got up from my chair and started putting the gun together.

"An animal, sir."

I hadn't been very long in Africa but I had discovered that for some reason some people didn't like mentioning the name of some animals. It often made conversation difficult but it was no use getting upset about it. One just had to guess and go on guessing until one hit on the answer. This was complicated in my case by a rather limited vocabulary.

"Is it a polecat?"

It wasn't a polecat. I had started with this because we had had one the week before in the chicken-run, and I remembered the word.

"Is it a leopard?"

"No, Bwana. It isn't a leopard." He used the word himself to show me what a silly question it was. No one, he clearly implied, minded using a word like leopard.

"Is it a rat?" I wondered if perhaps I had been overplaying this a little.

But it wasn't a rat either.

"Is it a . . .?" A horrid thought struck me. No. It couldn't be—this was a Saturday. This was the day for my lunch and a long sleep.

"Is it a . . .?" I hardly liked to use the word myself.

"Is it a snake?" I had got it out at last.

I knew at once that it was. Ali didn't even reply.

I picked up the cartridges and went with him down the steps into the courtyard. My stomach followed me, a few paces behind.

My cook then was an elderly, morose man. He was quite a good cook, but he was a man of the town, and he didn't like the country or the things that lived in it. He had shut and locked the kitchen door and was muttering to himself under a coconut tree.

When I told him to open the kitchen door he shook his head and rolled his eyes. He was quite honest about it.

"I am frightened," he said. I knew how he felt. I took the key from him and unlocked the door. But I didn't open it. I didn't somehow feel quite ready to start on Act Three. First of all I looked through the window. All I could see was cobwebs. I tried opening it, but it wasn't any use. I listened outside the door. Yes, there was a sound. It was rather like the engine of an old car being run on cheap petrol, but after a bit I realized that it didn't come from inside the room.

In the courtyard they waited and watched. I knew that I had to do it sooner or later. I put out my hand behind me for my courage, but I couldn't reach it. I slid the safety-catch and opened the door.

The smoky gloom of the kitchen contrasted strongly with the glare of the midday sun outside. I couldn't see a thing.

"Where was it?"

The cook edged forward a little. I could see the pipe curling up above the stove. The hole in the wall had been plastered once but most of it had fallen out and now there was a jagged gap. I couldn't see any sign of life at all, there or anywhere else.

I moved the gun slowly until I had the hole well covered. I took a deep breath for confidence. But all I got was smoke.

The kitchen had been put up on the cheap many years before and the walls weren't very solid. When I fired, plaster and rubble billowed out into the room in heavy enveloping clouds. I backed away as far as I could and waited for the air to clear. Suddenly there was a terrible noise.

"——!" I thought. "What have I done?"

Just before I reached the door I realized it was the pipe. I looked and saw it lying twisted in agony over the stove, its roots, red with rust, torn from the wall.

Behind me came a throaty duet of a whisper.

"Is it dead?"

It was ten minutes before they found the first bit. It looked like the jellied eel you buy in Petticoat Lane. They had been scratching about with long sticks, and in the end they found most of it. Out of curiosity we laid the pieces out on the ground in the courtyard and got a rough idea of what it must have looked like. The eyes had a reproachful look in them, and the tail still had a slight wriggle.

"What a shame!"

The voice of the stranger startled us. We were still a bit on edge. For a moment I thought it might be someone from the R.S.P.C.A.

But he didn't look that sort of person. His hair stood up in a frizz and his teeth were filed to a sharp incisive point. I had never seen him, or anyone like him, before.

"What a shame!" he repeated. "In so many pieces."

He bent down and rearranged our jigsaw with quick knowledgeable fingers. Now it looked much more like a real snake.

"The piece here," he pointed delicately. "Where is it?"

In a short time he was back with the missing section.

"It is the best bit," he explained.

He said something to Ali which I couldn't understand.

"What does he want?" I asked. I was beginning to feel sleepy.

"He asks if you will kindly allow him to take it away."

"Yes," I said. "Yes, indeed."

He scooped up all the pieces except one and put them carefully inside his shirt. He saluted me gravely and said "Thank you."

When I was halfway up the steps I turned and asked:

"Why do you want it?"

"Why?" He stared at me incredulously. "To eat, sir."

I had one more question. It was about the piece he had left on the ground. It was the tail, I had noticed.

Again he was incredulous at the silliness of the question.

"But no self-respecting man eats the tail," he said.

He shrugged his shoulders, and, with one hand clutching the precious burden inside his shirt, he made his way with dignity out of the courtyard, and I watched him until he disappeared among the trees.

CHAPTER SIX

A Goat for his Supper

IN THE evenings for exercise I used to walk along the strip of sand between the coconut palms and the sea. The District Commissioner also went for walks in the evening, not I think because he believed in exercise but because it made him feel, when he poured out his first whisky afterwards, as if he had earned it. Walking, he once told me, took the place of soda.

I had to be careful not to do my walking at the same place and the same time. If he saw me, and the distance and the direction were such that it was certain we wouldn't meet, he would wave in a happy and sociable manner, but in any other circumstances he would look the other way. If, as happened

c
33

once or twice before I learnt better, we actually met, he would scowl and mutter to himself as we passed.

I had a brindle bull-terrier then, and when I got tired of throwing sticks for him to retrieve from the water he would start digging for crabs. He would watch when they scuttled into their holes and then he would scoop furiously with his front paws. When he caught them he would bite their claws off until they lay limp and still. Sometimes he got nipped but he never yelped. He was killed later after a fight with a leopard when he was out one night chasing one of his numerous female friends. His name was Michael and he was a very fine dog.

That particular evening when I got back there was someone waiting for me. He had a letter tucked neatly in the fork of a stick. When I opened it I saw that the words were written in spidery Arabic script. It took me a long time to make them out. The first four lines were taken up with formal, mellifluous greetings and the last two lines were equally formal and equally mellifluous valedictions. In between was one sentence which contained the message.

About an hour later I sent back a reply saying I would be there early the following morning. This message was sandwiched between layers of politenesses. It was the custom.

The village was about three miles along the coast, and I walked. The path went through coconut trees all the way. The sun was rising over a flat glassy sea and the frigate birds were hovering waiting to pounce on smaller birds coming home from their fishing with their catches in their beaks.

I carried my shotgun on my shoulder. It wasn't loaded but I had a few cartridges in the pocket of my jacket.

The headman of the village had come some way along the path to meet me. It was he who had sent the message. He was a quiet-spoken, confident, self-contained man. He wore a white robe with a green scarf draped over one shoulder. His head was bound turban-wise with a yellow scarf. His ancestors had come many generations before from the bare jagged hills beyond the Persian Gulf to serve as guards and soldiers for the Arabs. The Arabs had been hard, lean, ascetic men but success and slaves and ease had sapped their sinews and their senses, and they called in others to protect them and what they had acquired and achieved.

We walked together through the village and out into the fields beyond where they grazed their stock. As we went others followed us, and by the time we reached the place there was a procession of coloured scarves and turbaned heads.

"It was here," he said.

There was a meadow of thin spiky grass. Along one side was a line of mango trees. On the other the ranks of coconut palms leant awkwardly away from the salty wind that came in from the sea.

There were still smears of blood on the grass and we could see where the cow had been dragged towards the mango trees and the bush that lay beyond them There was a faint musty smell that reminded me of the zoo.

"The lioness must have waited there in the bush," the head-man explained. "The boys were rounding up the cattle with their sticks for the night, but this cow was obstinate. She stayed to graze on, and it was then that the lioness came out in a quick purposeful rush and killed her."

"What did the boys do?" I asked.

"They shouted and waved their sticks but the lioness took no notice of them. She dragged the carcass of the cow past the mango trees into the bush. Then she dropped it and advanced towards the boys, snarling. They were frightened."

"Yes," I said.

"They herded the other cows together and drove them back to the village. They watched the lioness over their shoulders, but when she saw that they were not coming after her or the carcass she sat down on her haunches and waited there until they were out of sight. When the boys got back to the village and told us what had happened I collected some men and we came here."

"What did you have?" I asked. "What weapons?"

"Sticks. We had some sticks. And spears—and my gun."

I knew his gun. It was an old muzzle-loader. It was a beautiful and ancient piece but it didn't always work.

"But," he went on, "by the time we got here it was too dark to see. We had a lamp but we could not follow the spoor or the traces of blood. In the end we went home."

Four days later, he told me, the same thing happened again. That was on a Tuesday, three days ago.

By the time I came back that evening they had built the stockade and inside it, apprehensive already, was a goat. I had left my gun with the headman, and the village expert was still working on the mechanism of the trap.

"How goes it?" I asked.

"Well," he replied, "with God's help it will work."

He was a wizened, bent old man with a finely drawn, pale-skinned face. Kneeling on the ground beside him was a girl smoothing the kinks from a length of cord between her fingers. Her hair was straight and there was a hint of the Semite in the curve of her nose, but her skin was very dark.

"Her fingers are more supple than my sons'," he explained.

"Is she your daughter?"

"Yes. Of my seven daughters and four sons she is the most accomplished.

"Give it to me now," he said to the girl. He took the cord and ran it between his fingers.

"It is good. Now tie it to the stick."

The stockade was made of branches dug well into the ground and laced with thorn bush. There was an opening about four feet high and a couple of feet across. The earth had been scooped out in the entrance and a stick fixed in sideways at the base of the hole. The girl tied one end of the cord to it and when it was secure she filled up the cavity with stones and earth until it was flush with the ground.

My gun was wedged in the branches above the entrance, the barrels pointed directly down towards it. The old man took the cord from his daughter and threaded it over a notch he had cut in a branch above the stock.

"Grease it," he told the girl. She rubbed the grease into the notch of the wood and on the cord where it passed over it.

The old man turned to me.

"Which barrel will you use?"

I put a dummy cartridge in the choked barrel and showed them the trigger that went with it.

He took the cord himself then to test the pressure and to gauge exactly where the knot should be. He marked it with his nail.

"Now tie it there," he ordered the girl in a harsh uncompromising voice, but he rested his hand on her shoulder while she tied the end of the cord to the trigger.

The cord now was drawn taut, but not too taut, in a line up the middle of the entrance. He pushed at it with a stick until, running over the notch, it moved the trigger. But the pressure wasn't right and he told the girl to undo and then retie the cord. When he had got it right I broke the gun and replaced the dummy with an S.S.G.

The goat watched these events with apprehensive eyes and a continual bleat. It was tethered so that it couldn't nudge the cord from inside and spring the trap.

"Whose goat is it?" I asked the headman.

He coughed.

"It is a stray goat," he said after a longish pause.

I thought it better to leave the matter there. We had, for the moment, other things to worry about.

We climbed into the tree about an hour before it got dark. There were three of us altogether. The headman had brought a boy of about sixteen with him. He was an effeminate-looking creature with long curly hair and a cast in one eye.

"He is good with a knife," the headman explained. The boy carried a machete in a leather scabbard held on a belt round his waist.

When it got dark the goat bleated more loudly and more piteously than before. But apart from that it was very quiet. In the distance I could hear the sea lapping the sand in a slow regular rhythm, and from the village half a mile or so away there came sometimes a cry or a laugh. But not very often. They were for the most part waiting and listening as well.

There was no moon, but I had a luminous dial on my watch. It was ten past nine when we first heard the noise. The headman put his hand on my arm and I could feel the pressure of the fingers as he listened and calculated where and what it was. After a bit I felt his fingers relax.

"A jackal," he whispered. "Only a jackal."

The tree we had climbed and used as our vantage-point was about sixty yards from the stockade. When my eyes got used to the darkness I could just make it out against the background of the coconut palms. The goat, wearied no doubt by much fruitless bleating, was quieter now, and there were no more noises from the village.

At first I couldn't make out whether it was real or not. The sound seemed to come from the mango tree next door to ours. I thought I must have imagined it until I saw that the other two had turned their heads towards the noise as well. I knew I had heard that noise before and suddenly with a rather sickening jab of memory I realized what it was. It was the noise a cat makes when it tests its claws on the bark of a tree. It wasn't very loud, but once I recognized the likeness it became more and more distinct.

I saw the boy nod his head and I knew then that the lioness had come back after all. A thin moon was beginning to come up but it was still very dark, and I couldn't make out any shape or movement through the thick foliage of the tree. A few minutes later the boy whispered, "She has gone. Over there." He pointed towards the bush away from the direction of the stockade. I hadn't heard anything but I didn't doubt that he was right.

We waited for a long time after that. The moon climbed slowly up the stems of the palms but it was misted and there wasn't much light from it. I looked at my watch and saw that it was nearly one.

I remember that when I was a small boy I was sleeping in a strange room in an attic. For no reason at all it seemed I woke up and, without evidence of sight or sound, I suddenly knew there was something else in the room. It was only a friendly household cat that had come in through the window, but I still remember the moment of fear between knowing something was there and knowing what it was.

It was no more at first than a sense that there was something on the branch above us. I couldn't hear anything nor, when I looked up, could I see any movement or shadow. The other two were watching the stockade, and I knew somehow that I had to deal with this on my own.

I tried to force down my numbing empty-making fear, but it stayed inside me until I could almost see the dark mass of the lioness in the tree and hear the brush of her hide as she crawled slowly along the branch. And then moving my head slightly I saw the eyes.

The boy must have been watching me. He made a quick animal noise with his tongue, there was a sudden silent movement and a quiet quick rush of air, and it was gone before I saw what it was.

A few moments later the headman put his hand again on my arm. The pressure was very slight, and he just moved one finger to show me where to look.

I had never seen a lion before outside a zoo, and at first it looked much smaller than I had expected. It was still too dark to see anything except the shape, but the lithe cat-like movement, the slow advance and then the sudden frozen pause were unmistakable.

The goat was bleating in panic and tearing at its tether. When the lioness was about twenty yards from the stockade she seemed to make up her mind that the coast was clear. She walked slowly still but without pause or hesitation straight to the stockade.

She walked round it first of all, and then finding no easy way in she tried the fencing. The thorns pricked her and she shook her head. She walked round the stockade a second time before she paused in front of the narrow entrance.

She pawed delicately and we feared that she would stretch

the cord and set the gun off while her head was still clear. The headman's fingers on my arm dug into me as he held his breath.

Quite suddenly the lioness made up her mind. It was as if she sensed or smelt that man had tampered with the stockade and she started to walk away. But just then the goat, which seemed to have been paralysed into silence while these close operations had been going on, let out a frantic bleat. It was too much for the hungry lioness.

She turned and went straight in with a quiet angry snarl. The noise of the gun burst on the silence of the night with shattering reverberating violence.

Almost before my ears had recovered from the impact the boy had slid down the trunk of the tree and was running towards the stockade. The thin moon just caught the metal of the machete in his hand.

We slid down too but much more slowly. We were still some way away when the boy picked up a stone and threw it at the shape of the lioness on the ground. It didn't move and he went right up to the body.

"It's dead. It's dead," he shouted.

And indeed it was. The heavy cartridge had blown a great hole in the neck and the lioness was very still.

Away in the village we could hear the noises of excitement and jubilation. They would have heard the shot and the boy's shouted verdict. Already we could hear them coming along the path through the coconut palms, their cries and laughter clear in the quiet stillness of the night.

I slipped the gun away from the wedges, and when I had extracted the spent cartridge I dropped it on to the ground beside the body of the lioness. The boy bent and picked it up.

"Why do you do that?" I asked.

He smiled but he wouldn't say anything.

The headman provided the answer.

"He will give it to his girl. She will wear it as a talisman on her ankle. For luck," he added with a laugh.

While we were speaking the boy was kneeling over the lioness. He had his knife and was cutting at one of the paws. After a moment he stood up and stretched his open hand towards me.

"It is for you," he said.

It was a claw, bloody still from where he had cut it from the paw. I put it in my pocket, wondering if this, too, was meant for luck in love.

When the people from the village had arrived and examined the lioness, and when they had dissected the night's events to their satisfaction, we set off back to the village.

I still had one question curled up uncomfortably inside me. But I didn't like to ask the boy. I waited until he was out of range.

"Do you remember," I asked the headman, "just before you saw the lion something moved on the branch above us?"

"Yes," he said. "I remember."

"Do you know what it was?"

"Yes," he replied. "I saw it."

"What was it?" I asked. My voice had sunk to a low whisper.

"It was an owl."

He saw the surprise and the shame on my face and to soften the blow he added that owls sometimes had very nasty claws.

Ahead of us, leading the procession, was the goat led on a string and bleating now on a happier note. He at least, I thought, deserved the meal that was waiting for him in the village.

CHAPTER SEVEN

Two Hundred Shillings for the Sultan

I ALWAYS knew he was coming long before he actually arrived in my office. Stir flowed from wherever he was like ripples in a pond. The messengers in the corridor outside would start whispering. Any other people who happened to be there would shuffle their feet and back against the wall. I would hear the distinctive, confident flap of his sandals as he came up the steps, and the swishing of his robe as he gathered up the hem against the dust.

I always stood up when he came into my office. When he shook hands, he would first grasp my thumb in an Islamic clasp before taking my hand in both of his. It was like being embraced by a pair of warm soup-plates.

Then, duly invited, he would settle himself in a chair. People waiting in the corridor to see me would move away into

43

the harsh sunlight in the courtyard to come back another time. They knew it was no use waiting. The Sultan was there and he always stayed a long time.

He wasn't really a Sultan but that's what everyone called him. He had in his time been one of the most powerful and the most respected chiefs in the country, with a quarter of a million people in his charge. He was a man of authority and though it was many years since he had been deposed he still looked the part. He was of royal blood, and even his excesses and his indiscretions were part of the royal pattern. There was a lot of the Tudor in the Sultan.

"Well," I would say, to make things easier for him, "would an advance of a hundred shillings help the situation?"

He was not a man to beat about the bush, and I soon learnt that it was better not to pretend that he had come to see me about anything else.

"It would help . . ." he agreed. It was clear from his voice that a good deal more than that was needed to deal with this particular situation.

Since he had been dethroned and exiled to live here on the coast he had been given a monthly allowance of thirty pounds. Thirty pounds in 1936 in Bagamoyo was quite a lot of money. It was certainly more than I lived on. But the Sultan had a wide range of expenses that I didn't have.

As far as I remember he only had one wife with him, but he had a lot of friends.

I was his banker, more or less. If he wanted an overdraft he came to me—about once a month that was, on an average.

He drew his chair a little closer. He let his chain of amber beads lie in his lap. His hands thus freed, he was ready to talk. He had a fine deep voice and a fluent, mellifluous eloquence, but it was with his hands that he really made his points.

44

"Women," he said, and his hands seemed to embrace a multitude of them, "women always bring trouble."

"Yes," I said, "truly."

"It is fortunate that I am an old man. I am not bothered with them much."

I wondered where this unusual line of argument was leading to.

"As you know, whenever any of my people come to this town they come to my house. It is the custom."

He had switched the point of attack, I saw. I wondered why.

"Mostly they are men. Traders in cattle, or men from the big town usually when they are in some sort of trouble. I feed them and give them a place to sleep. Sometimes I give them money to help them."

I knew this was true. This is what he had done in his big house at Itetemia when he had been Chief. And as his father had done before him. Livingstone, who had lived close to this big house, had known this too and commented on it.

"A few weeks ago a woman of my people came to my house. A young girl."

He let this point sink in. He took up his beads again. This was obviously the interval.

He edged his chair a little closer. But it was not, as I had thought, for greater proximity and an incursion into indelicate detail. It was for the spittoon. I always kept one for visitors, particularly in the holy month of Ramadhan when spitting was very U in Muslim Bagamoyo. Like Henry the Eighth, the Sultan was used to spittoons in his stateroom. He also, I am told, in his prime had draught beer in his bedroom. As equally King Henry did.

Refreshed, he continued.

"She had run away from her husband, a Swahili, a man of

the coast," he added with a touch of contempt in his rich landed-up-country-gentry voice.

"The girl has been in my house for some time, and now she"—he sketched the situation with a modest shrugging of his hands—"and now she wants to stay."

"Ah," I said.

"The husband wants to make trouble—big trouble."

"Have you . . .?" I asked. "Did you . . .?"

"Of course." He dismissed the possibility of a negative answer with contempt.

"She is a girl who knows how to show respect," he added, to make matters clear.

Adultery is not commonly regarded in Africa as a cause for divorce. It is a matter for a civil claim for damages. Substantial damages sometimes, especially if the offender is a man of substance, like, for example, a retired Sultan. Claims of this sort filled the records of the Chiefs' and Headmen's courts and were the most common cause of litigation. It is not a bad system, but there were people who abused it. I knew of some elderly gentlemen in the District long past their prime who invested in wayward young wives beyond their capabilities in much the same way as men in England invest in equities. Instead of raking in the dividends and capital increase they pursued claims for adultery and added the children to their household.

This husband too wanted to sue the Sultan for damages. I knew from experience what they were likely to be.

"Will you deny the charge?" I asked.

It was a silly question, and he treated it with the disdain it deserved.

"Deny it? Of course not. I have a reputation to keep up."

"Yes," I said meekly. "Yes, of course."

"I have a different suggestion." He drew his chair up again. This time it was for business. "I know the girl's father. He is one of my people. The husband has paid him ninety shillings as the bride-price for the girl. This is on account. There is still another sixty shillings to be paid.

"If I pay him this sum of money, a hundred and fifty shillings, he thinks he could persuade the husband to drop the claim and to release the girl."

"You mean he would repay the husband the ninety shillings?"

"Exactly," said the old man.

"And keep the rest . . .?"

"Of course." He was getting a bit impatient with my obvious questions.

"I see," I said.

"So—if you could advance me the money—say two hundred shillings . . ."

I thought about this for a bit. Seeing my hesitation he moved his chair closer again. Just a little, but enough to let him lay his hand on my arm.

"In the long run," he said, "it may be cheaper than a claim for damages. Besides," he added, "the girl is useful in the house."

In the end I turned in my chair to call the clerk who did the accounts. But before I called I turned to the Sultan again.

"Yes," I said, "but why two hundred shillings? Would not a hundred and fifty . . .?"

"I would like to give the girl a present, naturally."

"Yes, naturally," I said. And I called the cashier.

CHAPTER EIGHT

The Green and White Striped Cloth

OUTSIDE the office there was a row of pegs. The first time I went into it I saw the piece of green and white cloth hanging on the end peg. I wondered what it was.

Most of the people who came to my office were from the town, or from the villages up and down the coast. They wore coloured shawls and scarves on the shoulders of white blouses, and striped skirts modestly worn to well below the knee. Their sandals were made from discarded lorry tyres. Their problems were the problems of the Ten Commandments, and they quarrelled fiercely over the division of fractions of fractions of exhausted coconut trees. They had nice, slightly ostentatious manners. They turned their heads aside to spit. They were very likeable people.

Most of my visitors were men. When, rarely, a woman had a problem or a proposition for the Government, she came enveloped in relations and yards of brightly coloured cloth. It was the custom.

One day I asked who the green and white cloth on the peg outside the door belonged to. They told me that it had been put there by the Lady of the Big Hat "for a purpose . . ." It was clear from their voices that it was sacrosanct; not to be questioned or spoken lightly of.

Later, when no one was looking, I fingered it gingerly as I passed. The green and white stripes took shape as a woman's frock. "The Lady of the Big Hat," I had discovered, was the wife of one of my predecessors. I wondered again why it was there. But I didn't remove it.

Late one evening a message came through from the headman of a place called Gawa or something like that. It was in the hills many miles away. It was a laconic message. It said:

"There has been a murder. The killer has an axe and he is angry. Please send many many police with guns."

Early next morning I set off. I had not yet visited this area. The road was not very good and it was late afternoon by the time I arrived.

Everything looked very peaceful. The headman explained that the killer had changed his mind and was not angry any more. The man himself stood there against the wall of the hut. He was an oldish man with a kind, benevolent face. Round his middle there was a piece of string and hanging from it, slightly askew, was a small leather apron. He also had an old army hat. Only the headman, who wore a long shirt and a solar topee of Edwardian manufacture, and the clerk who wore khaki shorts and shoes, were dressed. It was very hot up there and the people were conservative. Clothes had not yet come to Gawa.

In the hut where it had happened I drew some little maps and paced the floor to get the distances right. The killer was very helpful and moved things out of the way for me. The High Court seemed to like little maps drawn to scale in murder cases. The corpse I put in the back of my station-wagon. She was very dead, but again the High Court liked to have these things confirmed by a doctor. We wrapped up the head in a piece of sacking and put it on top of the body. The axe I kept in the front with me.

The killer shook hands all round and we set off for home. On the way he explained that he had come home one evening. He had been out hunting. His wife was asleep. She was blissfully and completely drunk. The fire was out. There was no food. She had drawn no water from the well. The baby hadn't been fed for hours and was crying angrily on the floor. He was, as he said, upset. He reached out his hand for some convenient means of waking his wife.

"Unfortunately," he sighed, and shrugged his shoulders, "it was an axe. I must have hit her harder than I meant to."

In the back of the station-wagon the head rolled slightly as we negotiated a slalom of potholes.

By the time we got back it was long past his bedtime. He was fast asleep with his head on the shoulder of his escort. His apron was still slightly askew.

Some days later I was sitting in my office trying to add up a column of figures. I was not very good at adding and it required a lot of concentration. Noises off in the corridor outside had been building up for some time. Suddenly they erupted. A small riot, I thought, or perhaps a snake. I was nearly at the end of the column.

By the time I went out into the corridor to see what was happening the riot had changed into farce. Everyone was helpless with laughter. There was a woman, a sturdy, strongly built figure but undoubtedly a woman. She was surrounded by my messengers and clerks, and when I arrived they had got it as far as what we usually call the hips. One more pull, one more co-operative wriggle, and the job was done. Dressed in the green and white striped frock the woman turned and made her way to my office. She looked terrible.

She was from Gawa. The axe, she explained, belonged to her. She had lent it to her sister (now deceased) to chop firewood. She pointed at it accusingly. It lay on a shelf behind me, and it was marked "Exhibit C."

Our talk lasted for some time. As, empty-handed, she stalked out of my office, she started to pull the frock over her head, as if to show me that she at least had a proper respect for other people's property. I noticed that round her waist she wore the girdle of beads worn by unmarried girls in the hills.

I went out into the courtyard and watched the dark sturdy figure walk away towards the trees. The single row of beads glinted in the sun. Her grace and dignity and modesty were beautifully restored. They had all been singularly absent in my office.

I went to the row of pegs and took down the green and white striped cloth. I called for some paraffin and we burnt it in the yard.

As the smoke drifted upwards and towards the sea my oldest messenger clucked his tongue and shook his head.

"The Lady of the Big Hat, God rest her soul, will be turning in her grave."

"But," added a younger man, "the Master, her husband, if he still lives, he will be laughing like a horse."

CHAPTER NINE

The Fly-Switch

WHEN I left Bagamoyo I was given a present. It was given to me by the ex-Sultan whose money and other troubles had often taken up so much of my time. But it was never wasted time. From him I learnt more about the mystique of authority in Africa than from anyone else.

A few weeks before we had been sitting together as guests at a *ngoma* in the town. *Ngoma* covers a multitude of activities and a multitude of sins, but roughly it means a party. It was held in a sort of square under tall, leggy coconut palms which had been planted at about the same time as Livingstone had set off on his journey to the Great Lakes. And it was from Bagamoyo that he had started.

The party consisted mostly of communal dancing and communal singing, but from time to time small groups of men and girls would detach themselves to mime a play or an incident. One of these took place round a table and a chair. The chair was empty, and the only thing on the table was a fly-switch. It was just a piece of stick with a few strands of hair attached to it.

I asked what it was.

The ex-Sultan didn't reply at once. Then he leant towards me and explained.

"It is a sort of play. To show what happens when you go to see the D.C. Because you are here, there is no one playing the part of the D.C. If you were not here there would be someone in the chair with a large sun-helmet on his head and a pipe in his mouth."

"I see," I said, ". . . and the fly-switch?"

"The D.C. always carries a fly-switch. It is, for the people here, a symbol. A symbol of power."

When a few days later he came to say good-bye, he was carrying a fly-switch. But it was not just a piece of stick with strands of hair as the other had been. The handle was covered in leather and worked with a design of Arabic characters and it had a fine silken black brush taken from the tail of a kudu. It was a beautiful thing.

"It is for you," he said. "When you are older and more important, you will need a symbol of authority. Something that everyone will know and recognize. Simple country people expect it, and in their hearts they want it. So take it, with my blessing, and in time, if you act justly and wisely and, if need be, firmly, it will become so well known and so respected that if you merely leave it on the ground or hang it on a tree people will know that authority and peace and justice are there. Even if for the moment you yourself are many miles away."

So I took it, and after that I always or almost always carried it with me.

Many years later, by an odd coincidence, I was given charge of the very District from which the old Sultan came and where he himself had once ruled. One of his sons had by then been installed as Chief, and he had the same dignity and authority and perception that his father had had. And him too I liked and respected very much. He is dead now, by his own hand.

Once in a very distant and unfrequented part of that District I lost the fly-switch. It fell out of my car when I was driving along a track. Weeks later it was returned to me.

"Someone found it," they said, "and knew it was yours."

I was glad to get it again. But in my heart I knew that it had come back not because it was mine but because they knew in every corner of that huge acre who had given it to me.

CHAPTER TEN

To Another Place

AFTER a year at Bagamoyo I was posted to another District. It was called Kiberge.

The idea, I suppose, was that I should gain experience of different areas and different races. Although people, even in Tanganyika itself, now think of what is called Tanganyika Territory as an entity, it is in reality an entirely fictitious creation and it has no homogeneity whatsoever in people or geography or climate. It was in fact drawn on the map in London and Berlin by people who had never been there and couldn't have cared less. The lines drawn cut across established areas and boundaries in a thoroughly unsporting way so that some tribes found themselves being governed half by the Germans and half by the British or the Belgians or the Portuguese, and others were cut off from their grazing grounds and their water supplies. Mount Kilimanjaro itself and the country round it was included in Tanganyika, and not in neighbouring Kenya, because Queen Victoria wanted to give it to her grandson Kaiser William as the dear boy was so interested in its fauna and flora.

The result was that what we now know as Tanganyika, which is about the size of France and Switzerland and Italy put together, has everything from hot sweaty swamp to snow-covered mountains, and peoples who have less in common with one another in looks and language and customs than the Eskimo and Cockney.

There was a lot to be said therefore for gaining new experience. One clearly had a lot of ground to cover.

The townsmen of Bagamoyo tended to regard people who lived twenty miles inland and wore fewer clothes as savages. These people in turn looked on the people who lived in places as far distant as this new District and who wore even fewer clothes as quite unspeakable. I quickly came to realize however, that although paucity of clothing may be regarded as a criterion of civilization and modesty in Europe it wasn't always a valid one in Africa.

As at Bagamoyo there were two of us in this other place. The D.C. was, however, an entirely different sort of person. Up to the end of the twenties men were recruited for the Colonial Administrative Service mainly from individualists who were bored with routine and slow promotion in the Army, or the Navy, from those who had acquired some experience of Africa in other fields, like the British South African Police, and from men who although they had failed to reach the sixth forms of the better-known public schools had some useful relations and a liking for an outdoor life. But then largely as a result of the stimulus and imagination of a man called Ralph Furse at the Colonial Office recruits began to be drawn from the universities. There were no exams and plenty of interviews, and the system and the nature of the job gradually attracted some of the best people Britain and the Dominions had or have ever had to offer. My new D.C., who had been at Trinity College, Dublin, and at Oxford and was one of the largest and finest Rugger internationals Ireland has ever produced, was one of them. I once listened to the broadcast of an Ireland v.

Wales match at Cardiff with him, and as I watched his enormous hands reminiscently opening and shutting during a line-out I was glad I had never played for Wales.

I lived for a year with him and his lovely Irish wife in this new District, and apart from a few missionaries there were no other Europeans in an area almost as large as Ireland itself. There was a lot of ground to cover and here too it wasn't very often we were both in the station together.

The D.C. had a pleasant little house made of burnt brick. Mine was of mud and wattle, like the huts in the village below the hill, but larger.

One way and another it was a very good year.

CHAPTER ELEVEN

My First Elephant

WHEN I first went out to Africa I used to listen with great respect to other people's stories of their first elephant. If I shut my eyes I can still see the long, curved bar at the Dar-es-Salaam Club, the shadows of the fans playing mercilessly on the damp, glistening bald heads of the older members, and I can still hear the stories that always ended, "And down he went, old boy, like a bloody battleship."

This new District I went to was very much up-country— "Out of the pink into the blue," as someone said as he drank his third gin-and-bitters and slapped me on the back.

I arrived in a lorry. There was a small village and up above it were half a dozen hills. Some of these had been cleared of the thick forest to make way for the forces of law and order. On one was the office and the flagstaff. On another was the District Commissioner's house. Farther away were the police lines, which looked across to another hill, on which, with a nice sense of fitness, the prisoners were building a new prison. On one of the hills was my house. Surrounding us was the forest, creeping back again wherever it got the chance.

One night I was woken by my factotum, Ali. He came in wearing an apprehensive expression and holding up a hurricane lamp. I looked at my watch. It was half-past two. He said that there was a crowd of people outside who wanted to see me on a most urgent and important matter.

"Must I go?" I asked.

"You must, sir."

"What do they want to see me about?"

"An elephant, sir."

Outside, in the dark and the drizzle, were about a dozen people. One of them who, in the daytime, typed my letters with three agile fingers and one enormous thumb, explained.

"In the valley below our huts are our gardens, our maize, our potatoes, our beans—our very life. An elephant is there eating and trampling. We have banged drums and our women have made horrible noises but he takes no notice. He goes on eating and trampling. Unless you shoot him all will be destroyed. Our wives will cry and our children will die of hunger."

Well, I thought, this is It.

"Relieve yourselves," I said.

I had slightly misplaced a Swahili vowel but, understanding, they just waited.

Inside my room, I thought desperately of a way out as I put on a very dark blue fisherman's jersey and a very dark pair of trousers. Inevitably, there was no way out. The only rifle I had was a very old Mannlicher I had bought for five pounds. But to impress I took my shotgun as well and a handful of No. 3 cartridges. As I appeared, armed to the teeth, there was an appreciative intake of breath.

"Let us go," I said, finding the right word this time, but not quite the confident ring.

As we walked in single file down my hill and up through the thick forest to the next, I wondered what on earth I was going to do. There was no moon and no stars. It was so dark I could barely see the man in front of me. We seemed to walk for miles.

At last the file stopped. One man whispered, "Listen." I listened. I could hear nothing but the cicadas and the pumping of my heart. "Look," he said. I could see absolutely nothing. After a bit the man again said, "Listen." This time I thought I could just hear dimly a munch-munch sound, away to the left. The faint sound grew inside me till it sounded like an elephant eating buns at the zoo.

I whispered, "You all wait here." I handed my rifle to Ali and took the shotgun. With unsteady hands, mercifully unseen in the darkness, I loaded it.

"Wait here," I whispered again. But now I spoke with decision. I had a plan.

I moved off to the left until I was sure that not even the cat's eyes of my supporters could see me. I waited—purely for effect. Then, lifting the shotgun until it pointed high in the sky and behind me, to be quite, quite sure that there was no possibility of irritating the elephant in his softest parts, I loosed off first one barrel and then the other. When the noise had stopped echoing away up into the mountains I listened. I could sense that everybody else was listening too; I could hear nothing at all.

Suddenly one of the men shouted, "He's hit him! He's hit him! Listen. He's going!"

I joined them quickly, just in case the elephant was going my way. Another man said, "He's gone! The elephant has gone."

I saw that standing next to me was a tall, gaunt figure wrapped in a blanket. He was one of my messengers, a man who always looked sad and who spoke rarely. He laid a hand on my arm and said with finality, "He has gone. I know it. I heard his ears flapping as he went." And I believed him.

As we returned, all the women and the children came running after us.

"He has killed the elephant!" they chanted and whinnied. In triumph I was escorted back to my house. I bade them good night. To Ali I said, "Bring the whisky."

Next morning Ali came in with the tea as usual at half-past six. As usual he put out my slippers and laid my clothes over a chair. As I sipped my tea he said, "Sir."

"What?" I asked.

"About that elephant."

"Yes," I said.

"They have seen the marks. It was a bush-pig. But," he added, "sir, it was a very, very big bush-pig."

CHAPTER TWELVE

The Goat it was that Died

"WELL," I said, "let's go."

I waited under the fig-tree while the porters picked up their loads of boxes and baskets and started off in single file down the narrow meandering path. On the horizon across the wide flat plain we could see the first streaks and flushes of the day's light, but up here in the trees on the slope of the hills it was still dark.

When Ali had finished beating out the embers of the fire he spat to make a final sizzle and we joined the tail of the column.

One always felt fine in the early morning at the start of the day's walking. It was cool and the air smelt clean and good. After a week of this sort of thing I was confident of my legs, and after the night's sleep I was fresh and untired.

It was nearly six o'clock before we reached the village and the camp which they had, more or less, brushed clean for our arrival. I said Hullo rather perfunctorily to the old Chief, and with even less ceremony to the others, and called for a basin of water and some tea.

While the village girls brought in their eggs and their curiosity I sat with my feet in the basin and started to take off the leeches.

It had been a long walk. For the last two hours the path through the swampy reeds had been under water and several times I had gone up to the waist in one of the soup-plate-sized depressions made by the hippo in the night. Most of the porters had taken off their clothes. This wasn't a dressy part of the world, but they were mostly strangers to the village, and to the children and the girls their arrival was rather like the visit of a mobile cinema with an X film.

Later that night they did a dance for us. I don't remember what particular kind of dance it was but they certainly seemed to have taken a leaf out of the porters' book in one respect. Some of the women wore their leaf on a cord of beads but the girls for the most part just wore the beads.

The village was built on a rise in the swampy ground but even on the flatter fringes of the rise the huts were perched on stilts. Twice a year in the rains the valley was flooded by the water that came down the river from the hills, and the people moved from place to place in small canoes hewn out of the trunks of trees. The goats were taken off by the young men on to the slopes of the hills, but the chickens stayed. They developed webbed feet, or so I was told.

I decided in the end to hear the Appeal in the evening. The people concerned in it were already there but I thought it would be interesting first of all to sit in as a spectator to some cases in the Chief's court. I wanted to see roughly how it worked.

Most of the litigation between Africans took place in these courts and one of our duties was to supervise them and if necessary to hear appeals from them. The courts did not use the formal procedures and codes which we were supposed to follow in our own courts. They used what was called Native Law and Custom.

It was an elastic term, as it was meant to be.

The Chief held his court, on the day I was there, in a small building of mud brick and thatched with reeds which had been built for this very purpose. Normally I believe he held his court under a group of mango trees, where there was much more room.

The case I listened to was about a goat. From all accounts it must have been an unusual animal, even for a goat. But it was difficult to say exactly. It had died about twenty years before.

"You see," explained the man, scratching his groin, "it belonged to my father. That, and six other goats."

"How did your father come to possess this goat?"

It was not the Chief who asked the question. It was one of the three assessors who sat with him—oldish men, gaunt and wrinkled with wisdom.

"It was like this." The man took a pace forward so that he was isolated from the others. "One of my sisters was married. A man called Kivunge took her. This goat was part of the bride-price."

"Ah," said the assessor. His voice was as brittle and as searching as a frigid wind.

"Eh . . ." he added as an afterthought. It was a more judicial noise than the one before.

Encouraged the man went on.

"But my sister did not like her husband. He beat her. After a year she went back to her mother."

"Who was her mother?" asked one of the other assessors.

The man looked up at the sky. He got no help there.

"I forget," he said.

"But you said the girl was your sister . . ."

"Yes." He agreed. "Same father, but a different mother. We did not know her——"

This was said in a tone of calculated offence. It was clear that this particular mother came out of a different and much lower drawer.

"Did your father return the goat?" This time the question didn't come from the assessors, or from the Chief. It came from the crowd. Justice, according to Native Law and Custom, was a very democratic process.

The custom here, as in many other places, was that the bride-price had to be returned to the husband if the girl left him.

The man scuffled his toes in the dust. After a longish pause he replied,

"A goat was returned. Truly, a goat was returned."

"That particular goat?" asked the man in the crowd.

No one spoke for some time. The Chief himself seemed to have dozed off. A village dog came amiably and aimlessly into the court-room and settled himself on the dusty floor.

It was the end of Scene One. No one was in a hurry to start the next scene, but they all knew what it would be and who would play the part.

When she appeared she took her cue as if there had never been an interval. She was a sinewy, leather-skinned old witch but her voice was rich and round like a barmaid's.

"No," she said. "No. It wasn't the same goat. It was the

same colour—the age was right. The size was exact. But it was a different goat."

For the first time the Chief asked a question.

"When the goat was sent back did you think it was the same?"

"Yes," the woman conceded in a voice that contained no syllable of surrender.

"When did you discover that it was not the same goat?"

"Not for several moons. Not until the female goats had young."

"And then——?" One of the assessors continued the questioning.

"I saw that the young goats were different. Different from the goats that the real goat, our goat, had fathered."

"That is no proof." An old man stood up in the crowd and gave his opinion. He looked like an expert on goats.

A murmuring started in the crowd. "She agrees. She agrees," they were saying. But the woman still held the floor and there was still no retreat in her stance.

"I will give you my proof," she said. "When I saw the young goats that were born I went to watch the other goat. I watched his manner of mating.

"Our goat mated like this . . ."

The demonstration was done with a few economical gestures. But they were enough. I now knew exactly the manner of it.

"This other goat . . ."

The new demonstration was quite different. It was very detailed and it was very funny. It was some time before the proceedings could be resumed.

"So," concluded the old woman, "we took this other goat back and asked for our own. They refused. Three times they refused. And so we went at night and took it, leaving the other in its place . . ."

The old Chief summed up there and then. Each point he put to the crowd, and not until he had got the murmurs of assent that he sought did he go on to the next.

In the end he gave judgment against the woman. She spat in the dust but she didn't dissent.

I didn't say anything during the proceedings but afterwards I asked the Chief about two things which had worried me.

The answer to my first question was easy.

"The father of the girl died. The son, the man who claimed the goat, was away and they waited until he returned."

It was twenty years before he returned, but there were, it appeared, no refinements like the Statute of Limitations in Native Law and Custom.

The other question was more complicated.

"Well, Bwana," he said, "it is true that the goat is dead and he cannot recover it. But that," he continued, looking down at his feet, "that is not the point. It was a question of principle."

The Appeal which I heard later that day was a different sort of case. It had been heard originally in the court of a minor Headman of a group of isolated settlements in the most inaccessible part of the swampy plain. They were unsophisticated people. They had been but barely affected by whatever had happened in the world outside their particular corner of the valley.

The case itself was a simple one in essence, but its complex elements were as old as man himself.

A man had a wife. After a time his wife became unwifely. He beat her, but she got no better. So he went to an old woman who, for want of a better word, could be described as a diviner of matrimonial causes. The old woman said that the trouble was that the girl was being unfaithful. What was more she was being unfaithful with one of his own brothers.

When he accused the girl she denied it. The brother also denied it. So he took the matter to court. As there were no witnesses the Headman did what his father and his father's father had done before him. He decided the matter by ordeal.

Trial by ordeal, which was still practised, I believe, in the more rural parts of England up to our grandfathers' time, takes many forms. It is in effect a kind of lie-detector.

In this particular case it was a boiling-water test.

"How was the test carried out?" I asked.

The old man who had supervised the thing stood up. But I told him to sit down. I thought it would be interesting to hear it from the girl herself.

She was a short, rather bow-legged girl of about sixteen. She wore a bunch of leaves, not very well centred, held by a cord round her waist and a string of coloured beads round her neck.

"There was a pot of water." She pointed to an open earthen-ware bowl about eighteen inches deep. "They set it over a fire until it boiled. Then they dropped a pebble in it. I saw it lying there in the bottom of the pot.

"Then that man," she pointed to the old man whom I had told to sit down, "asked me, 'Did you sleep with your husband's brother?'

"I shook my head. He said, 'Answer in words.' I said, 'No.'

"Then he said, 'Put your hand in the water and take out the stone.'

"I refused. I knew the water would scald me.

"He got angry. 'If you refuse you will be proved a liar,' he said.

"I said nothing.

"Then the man said, 'If you are speaking the truth you need have no fear. The water will not scald you.'

"So I put my hand in the water. It scalded me. I could not reach the stone. I took my hand out and ran away into the bush . . ."

On the basis of this evidence the adultery was held to be proved. The husband's brother was made to pay damages of two goats for the offence.

The next day the old Chief walked with us to the limits of his province. The case that I had heard had gone first to his own court on appeal, and he had upheld the decision. It was from this ruling that the Appeal to me had been made.

He knew that I had allowed the Appeal and quashed the case. But he didn't mention it. We talked about the rice they planted in the swamp and of the damage that the hippo did.

In the end I raised the subject myself. I asked him if he really believed that the girl had committed adultery.

"I don't know," he said at once. "I think she did, but I don't know."

"Why do you think so? Because of the hot water?"

"No, Bwana. I do not attach any importance to the water . . ."

He knew what my next question would be and he touched my arm before I asked it. I followed him to a slight rise in the flat ground where there was a solitary tree. From there we could see the whole arc of the swamp spread out like a fan. Here and there were huts and small villages in a few fields that had been cleared of reeds. But most of it was empty and flat and asleep.

"The people who live here," he said, "are few. They are

poor and ignorant and afraid. Always they are afraid. Their life is precarious and short and full of uncertainties.

"The thing they desire most is stability. They are afraid of change. Their customs and beliefs have been evolved over generations. Some of them may be strange to you and even to me. Some of them are harsh, and others are cruel. But they have stood the even harsher test of time and they are fitted to these people as a glove becomes fitted with much wearing to the hand . . ."

He didn't say any more. And in the end I didn't ask any more questions.

We said good-bye on the slight ridge which was the boundary of his country. He waited there until we were out of sight.

I let the others go on ahead. It was easy to follow the track of the porters, and I wanted to think.

One of the things I thought about was the ancient British custom of trial by jury. The more I thought about it the more it seemed to have in common with other, and even older, customs. It might not always produce the right answer, but it worked, and somehow it fitted. Yes, it fitted us like a . . .

Immersed in these thoughts I tripped over a hidden root and, deservedly, fell flat on my face.

CHAPTER THIRTEEN

The River

THE canoes were drawn up close to the bank of the river. They looked solid enough, I thought. They had been hewn and shaped out of the trunks of trees. The marks of the adze-like tool the local people used could be seen on the outside of the canoe. Inside they had been smoothed by rubbing and by use. They were about twenty-five feet long.

I watched the boxes and the bundles being stacked in the second canoe. The four boxes of tax money, much-thumbed and much-counted shillings and copper and crumpled five-shilling notes, were put in the first canoe. It was in this one that I, with one of the askari and two paddlers, would travel down the river. They had rigged up a rough awning to keep the midday sun off the Bwana's head.

The askari was tying lengths of rope round the four money-boxes. He looped the rope carefully round the iron carrying-handles and knotted it. At the end of each length he tied a piece of wood. The wood was soft and spongy and light. It was useless as timber or firewood but it would float.

It was not my own idea but it made me feel very practical. "If," someone had explained, "you get tipped up by a hippo at least you can trace the money-boxes afterwards. Otherwise of course they'll dock it off your salary. If you get nipped by a crocodile in the process, they'll probably only make you pay half."

The sun was coming up over the hills. Parakeets were chattering in the trees around the clearing. Disturbed by a shifting of the shadows on the water, a heron took off awkwardly from a log and made his way with heavy measured wing-beats down the river. There was a chill in the air but it was clean and clear, except for the thin blue smoke of early-morning fires.

The chief of the tribe that had conquered and then held the headwaters of this African river for a few generations was tall and powerfully built. His father, he told me, had drunk the Water, and had fought and died against the Germans here. The Water was river water in a gourd. But it had been blessed and cursed and exorcized until, it was said, it made one immune from the German bullets. Many, like his father, had died in the fantastic bravery of their credulity.

He wished me a good journey and protection from all ills. When he invoked the name of God he used Arabic words. He was a Muslim, and a fervent one as I well knew from previous days sitting a spectator in his Court. Throughout the long hot morning he had been listening to claims and counter-claims and lies and counter-lies over goats and women and crops. At the end of each piece of evidence and argument he had spat. The sentences and periods of his judgments had been similarly punctuated. It was the month of Ramadhan, and in this holy month a good Muslim ejects even his spittle to keep his vow not to take either food or water until sunset. I knew and liked him well, and that evening I had teased him that he should follow that portion of his creed so exactly and yet boast he had five more wives than the maximum of four allowed him by the rules of the Prophet. He had replied as befitted a man of authority.

"In all things a man must be reasonable. To carry anything to excess is to be no better than a woman."

As he took my hand in both of his he had an afterthought. It was patently one that had been carefully planned but it was nicely done.

"Bwana," he said, "would you do a kindness for me? There is a girl here, a kinswoman of mine. She has been visiting her mother. Now she wishes to return to her husband in the town. Would you give her a place in your canoe that she may return safely and quickly to her home?"

The girl was standing a few feet away, her bundle ready at her feet. Her eyelids were lowered. Only her toes scuffling in the dust indicated that she had heard and was waiting for my answer.

We pushed off and as we caught the stream in the middle of the river the paddlers started to sing. On the riverbank the men raised their hands in farewell and behind them the women of the village whinnied and ululated. In front of me in the canoe the bare, passive shoulders of my passenger shone like polished wood.

For about four hours we went smoothly and quickly down the river. It was only a tributary but we were still close to the hills and the stream was strong. All the paddlers had to do was

73

to keep the canoe in the middle and follow the line of the stream round the outside of the bends.

The trees came down thickly to the edge of the river. It was very quiet and apart from the herons there was little sign of life.

The paddlers were still strangers. The askari was taking his responsibility for the money-boxes very seriously. The girl would, of course, only speak when she was spoken to. I read a book. Something unusual would be needed to break the tropical ice.

It came soon after we joined the big river. We were going round a long bend keeping right over to the far side to catch the current. Without warning a hippo floundered up from a submerged sandbank below a fallen tree. He had probably been asleep when the swish of the canoe a few yards away woke him up. Frightened he tried to get into deep water. Caught by the stream the canoe kept pace with him and was too fast for him to elude.

Suddenly he turned. First he tried to bump us and when this failed he tried to bite a chunk out of the side of the canoe. His mouth seemed enormous, and the inside of it was a naked indecent pink. The paddler in front was all elbows trying to back-paddle and brake the canoe.

I was petrified. This was something that had never actually happened to me before. For a moment, for several moments, I just couldn't move. I knew what I had to do but I couldn't do it. The askari's hands were trembling as he tried to load his rifle from the cartridge-belt round his middle. Forewarned by the chief, I was already loaded. At last I found the movement to take aim. The canoe was lurching with the swirl of water as the paddlers braked and the hippo surged to try and get his teeth into the canoe. But in the end I got in a shot.

The noise, I think, rather than the impact, made the hippo

snort and submerge. Whether I hit him I shall never know, but as we settled down again into the stream we saw that the crocodile sunning themselves on the sandbanks were sliding noiselessly into the river. One of the paddlers said they were catching the smell of blood as it came down the river with us. I was glad it was the hippo's.

During that first day we saw about fifty hippo. They would pop their heads up out of the water when they first heard us about two hundred yards away. After watching us for a while they would submerge. Up they would come again about a hundred yards away. Another quick look and down again into the river. The next time they would wait until we were within twenty or thirty yards. There were usually schools of four or five or six and they would come up the last time in a sort of ring-a-ring-o'-roses all round us.

After several encounters of this sort I found that the best method of keeping them from coming too close was to delay shooting until, so to speak, I could see the whites of their eyes. Shots at a greater distance didn't seem to bother them, and they would then become cunning and not come up again until we were only a few feet away.

I didn't shoot to hit them, and in any case the canoe was rocking in the fast stream. To hit and not to kill, I reasoned, might make the hippo angry and I was a peace-loving man. In any case I had been well brought up and to hit an animal when you couldn't follow him to kill, and to kill an animal when you couldn't eat him or even mount his head in an aunt's attic in Shropshire afterwards was very bad form.

At about five o'clock we made for a clearing in the trees and tied up below a shallow bank. As they were unloading the canoes I looked for the marks of the hippo's teeth.

Quite distinct from the marks of the adze used to shape the

canoe were scratches and furrows in the side. Most of them were old, but one or two looked unhealthily recent.

"All the canoes on the river have them," the paddler said. "That hippo wasn't very big or very brave. You should see them when they have little ones nearby."

I went to sleep early that night. It was my birthday and I dreamt of hippo hunting me in the long grass on Shotover.

The next day we set off early. The hippo were well-behaved and I noticed, as I had the day before, that they were creatures of fixed habits. Between ten in the morning and three in the afternoon they slept on the river-bed and rarely appeared on the surface of the river. Only in the early morning and the late afternoon did their heads appear to watch us.

So I concentrated on the crocodiles. Most of them were about nine or ten feet long, but occasionally there would be a monster, battle-scarred and heavy-lidded, lying on the mud or the sand. Sometimes we saw them fishing, going down with a swirl of the tail and coming up a moment later with a fish in between the ramparts of teeth.

I shot at them now and again. As far as I was concerned there was no good form about shooting crocodile.

The girl liked it when I shot at the crocodile. When they were hit she would clap her hands and laugh. She told us about a cousin of hers who was taken by a croc when he was drawing water. His wife was ill, she explained, as normally the menfolk on the river wisely leave the drawing of water to the women. The croc caught him by the arm and dragged him under the water. He lost consciousness, but later on he came to and found that he was in a hollow under the bank and just above the water-line. Crocodile like their meat good and high, so he had been stored there to mature. But he dug his way out and reached the riverbank above, and the crocodile was cheated of his supper.

The askari, who came from up-country where there were no rivers and no crocodiles, shook his head and clicked his tongue in disbelief. But the paddler said that even though it was a woman telling it, the story might be true.

In the evening, before we pulled into a small village for the night, there were some duck flighting down the river to settle on the sandbanks. There were garganey and whistling teal and pintail, and that night we all had a very good supper. I shot from the canoe and we would pick them up on the sand and from the surface of the water.

That night, sore from sitting, but otherwise at ease and content, I sat in a canvas chair outside my tent. The paddlers and the askari were chattering over a small fire. The river chuckled and gurgled as it slid past us, and downstream we could hear the hippo pulling and munching the long grass. From the hills across the other side of the river came the throaty grunting of a lion returning home after a successful prowl.

One of the men came up and said,

"The girl, Bwana. She wants to speak to you."

She hung her head and I had to ask her what it was she wanted.

"I am frightened," she said.

I didn't think somehow that it was on account of the dark, or the hippo or the lion, and in the end I let her put her blanket on the ground outside the front of the tent where everybody could see her.

I only had one more day on the river. The water was broader and deeper here and there were villages along the sides. The hippo had learnt to be more wary of men and they kept their distance. The crocodiles remained scornful and menacing. They lay all day on the sandbanks while the river birds hopped amongst them and picked the ticks delicately from their hides. Towards evening they cruised the river, their snouts pop-eyed, shining wet above the surface.

It was late in the afternoon when we reached the ferry which carried the cotton lorries across the river to the ginnery. My lorry was waiting there.

I said good-bye to the paddlers and we watched them turn the long canoes and start tacking up the river against the stream. It would take them nine to ten days to do the journey we had done in three.

When late that night we reached the town I asked the girl where her husband's house was. She looked blank, but I thought I saw the ghost of a smile at the corner of her eyes.

Irritably I asked the messenger,

"Where is her house?"

There was a longish pause. My irritation evaporated into a faint suspicion.

"She doesn't live here, Bwana," he replied.

"The Chief asked me to take her to her husband's house. He said it was here."

The messenger had good manners, and he didn't smile. He knew that I hadn't been very long in Africa.

"She has no husband, Bwana. She is"— he hesitated—"a sort of niece to the Chief up the river. When our journey is finished she will, with your permission, return to her home there."

After a pause he added,

"It will only take her a week."

CHAPTER FOURTEEN

Rabbit Pie

THE mission station sat on a ledge of the hillside peering a little anxiously, one always felt, at the hot, earthy African plain below. But it had been there a long time and the cypresses and blue gums they had planted when they first arrived gave it an established, well-rooted look. The road went up along a narrow ridge and when I came in sight of the red tin roof and the whitewashed walls I slowed down. I needed time to think again how I would approach the subject. It was, after all, a delicate matter.

I wanted some rabbits.

This District was infested with something that looked like

a horse-fly and was called a tsetse-fly. It lived on the blood of warm-blooded animals, which, whether we liked it or not, included both the missionaries and me. If it had merely pricked us all with its long, needle-like proboscis and sucked in a little blood no one would really have minded very much. The trouble was that it left a killing disease behind it as well. The brands of tsetse-fly in this particular District didn't affect us humans as they did in some other places, but they did affect cattle.

The result was that there weren't any cows.

This meant that for much of the year we didn't get any meat. In the dry season cattle were driven down from the healthy hills and by the end of their long journey they were well-muscled but eatable. In the rains the tracks were impassable. So we lived on wiry chicken and tensile goat.

That was how I came to be on my way to the Mission to beg or buy a couple of rabbits. As I drove along the winding, dusty road I had visions of lots of little rabbits—and of rabbit pie.

The trouble was to explain why I wanted them. The bearded Italian priest was a gentle old man. I knew he kept rabbits, but I didn't know how fond of them he was. To make matters worse he was a vegetarian. That was the first difficulty. The second was a question of sex. I wanted young rabbits and telling the sex of rabbits isn't as straightforward as it might seem. I didn't want to get involved with the bearded priest or the nuns in any complicated discussions or examinations on the subject.

When I had worked out a rough plan of campaign I drove on and stopped the car under the mango trees in front of the house.

They didn't get many visitors at the Mission and curious eyes had been following the approach of my car and its attendant plume of dust. By the time I arrived the bearded Italian was already there on the doorstep. He shooed away the crowd of cripples and orphans and acolytes and chickens which had collected in the courtyard. I saw the heavy lace curtains in the other building move and I knew the nuns were watching as well. "What has he come for?" they would be whispering in their liquid Latin voices.

I hid my present of a bottle of whisky as best I could, and followed him into the bare, cool room inside. There on a table already was a bottle of Algerian wine and four large tumblers. In the shadows two other priests were waiting.

They didn't normally drink when they were on their own, but when there was a visitor things were different. There was also, I saw, a small box of cheroots.

We didn't start on the bottle of whisky for some time. And it wasn't until they had all tasted it and commented politely on its excellence that I steered the conversation towards the subject of rabbits.

"The rains, they say," I began, "will be very bad this year."

"So?"

It was obvious that there was no great enthusiasm for the subject. However, I persisted.

"In Mbawa they have already started," I went on.

"In Mbawa," broke in one of the priests, "the people are very, very wicked. I have heard that when the new moon comes the girls there . . ."

I knew what was coming. I had heard it before. That line of conversation could never lead to rabbits. So I poured him another tumbler of whisky and tried another tack.

"How are your pigeons?" I asked the old priest with the beard.

This met with a much better response.

"Very well, thank you. A thousand thanks for asking. Would you care to see them?"

They were in the next room. There were twenty-seven of them and each one had a name, and a history. It was some time before we returned to the table.

"And your chickens?" I asked.

"They are well. They are having many children, thanks be to God."

This was better, I thought, but I didn't want to rush my fences.

"You used to have some mice," I said tentatively. I wanted to get the conversation away from birds and on to four legs.

"They are all dead. Eaten by the nuns' cats," he said sadly.

I thought I had better strike quickly before it was too late.

"And the rabbits; your pretty brown-and-white rabbits. How are they?"

In the end he gave me three rabbits. I am afraid I funked both the difficult points. I didn't say anything about eating them and I didn't raise the question of sex at all. I just hoped that on the law of averages one of the three would be different from the others. When I got home I found that it was. It was a hare, and he was a long way past his prime.

I had a box made for the rabbits and put it outside on the verandah. The house was a bit isolated and during the night the garden had a lot of visitors. Mostly small animals and delicate-treading gazelles, but sometimes there were rabbit-eaters like leopards and jackals, and of course there were always my neighbours in the village down below. One day I found a pretty black and yellow snake curled up in one corner of the box watching the two rabbits, who had retreated to the other corner, with an uncharitable look in his eye. In the end I put the rabbits inside the house in my bedroom.

I got the impression early on that the rabbits were of differ-ent **sexes**, but although they displayed, as the books say, they never did more than that, as far as I could see. Even allowing for the careful upbringing which they had obviously had in the Mission they seemed to me to be circumspect in their approaches to the point of stupidity. I was brought to the conclusion that if animals had to rely solely on instinct they would soon die out. A little tutoring must, I thought, be done at mother's knee.

When I had almost given up hope one rabbit, whom I had from observation thought to be the male, suddenly produced nine little rabbits on Empire Day. They were quite enchanting.

As they grew older I gave them names. They all had patches of brown on the white, or white on the brown, so they were fairly easy to distinguish. Nor was it as difficult as I had expected to decide on names for them. The faces or the habits of the rabbits, and sometimes both, quickly reminded me of people I knew. One was like an aunt and another I called H.E. Some I named after girls I had known in England and one, for reasons which will only be understood by a few, and which I cannot I'm afraid explain, was called the Crab. He was a very unusual rabbit. By and large, however, they had none of the shyness together of their parents, I noticed.

We were rather off the beaten track, and even when we did have visitors there were not many ways of entertaining them, especially if they were used to living in towns. The rabbits soon became Exhibit A for these visitors.

"Very jolly," they would say, "but why do you keep them?"

I would put on a poker face and say that they were for eating in the rainy season.

"How many have you eaten so far?" somebody once asked.

"Well . . ." I said, "none actually—but of course . . ."

"Yes, of course." They always said that. You could see in their eyes that they felt I had been in this outlandish place long enough. Then I would make up my mind to eat one of the rabbits. Just to show that really I had my feet firmly on the ground. But it was so difficult to decide which one . . .

Worse than any visitor was my own cook. He was a morose, cynical old man, who came from an unsophisticated part of the country where they ate almost anything. They even ate lizards, grilled slowly, and preferably alive, over a charcoal fire.

He would come sometimes in the evenings, when I was feeding the rabbits, and stand beside me. He never said anything but I noticed that he always came when there was left just the right amount of time he would have needed to skin and cook a small animal for my evening meal. After a bit he would shrug his shoulders sadly, and soon afterwards I would hear a chicken's final squawk, or the cook's heavy breathing as he opened yet another tin.

I used to look at the rain clouds hoping they would go before he would insist that the growing rabbits were big enough to eat. I had on one or two occasions to speak quite sharply to him. But just in time the skies cleared for good, and the stringy cattle came once more over the hills.

When the rains came again the following year I had forty-three rabbits. But by that time, of course, I had laid in a large stock of bully-beef and tinned sardines.

CHAPTER FIFTEEN

To England and Back Again

A<small>FTER</small> my first two and a half years in Africa I went to England on leave. Two of us, who between us had just enough mechanical knowledge to change a tyre and warm up a wet sparking-plug, drove someone else's station-wagon the two thousand five hundred miles down to South Africa. Unkind people say that Spanish police always work in pairs because one can read and the other can write. Even kind people said rather similar things about us on this trip.

From Cape Town we went by boat to Southampton. A sea voyage was rather heady stuff for two newly confirmed cadets fresh from the solitude of bush-stations. We travelled tourist class for rather less than it now costs to transport a bull-terrier, but even so the decks were full of elegant cotton frocks and long brown legs and we were bowled over like ninepins all the way from Cape Town until it started to get rough in the Bay of Biscay. If we didn't emerge with honour at least we avoided any commitments from which our few years' experience as public servants didn't enable us to escape.

It was raining when we arrived, and London was covered in a thick yellow January fog. It smelt and tasted wonderful.

After a month skiing in Norway I rented a thatched cottage on the edge of the Chilterns. The most unexpected thing about being back in England was that you found it difficult to believe that you had ever been away. England in that summer of 1939 seemed exactly as it had been when we left it in 1936, and although the menace of war hung over a few far-seeing people, it bore lightly on the familiar greens and browns and yellows of the countryside and not at all, as far as one could see, on the ways and minds of nine people out of ten.

A friend of mine with whom I shared the cottage started learning to fly and I tried to wangle an attachment to a Territorial battalion, but most of the time we just enjoyed ourselves, and the idea of war remained as remote and as improbable as the Africa we had left. When people asked me about it I found it as difficult to describe as a dream. However clear a dream may seem at the time, it always fades and blurs when I try to tell it, and it was the same then with Africa.

In July 1939 I went back. I had joined the Reserve of the King's African Rifles at the time of Munich but it was six months before I was released to join up. The time in between I spent largely in a hilly District in the northern part of Tanganyika. It was beautiful, exciting country, but I was fretful to get away and I remember less of it and of the quiet, handsome, pale-skinned people who lived there than I would have wished.

CHAPTER SIXTEEN

The Trace

IN THE early mornings I used to come out of the tent and drink my tea by the embers of the big brushwood fire. It was cold in the hills in the night and in the twilight before dawn, and I wore corduroy slacks and an old and slightly smelly fisherman's jersey.

The men slept in blankets and heaps round the other fires. As I drank my tea they would yawn and stretch their arms and hold their blankets across their faces against the wind as they went out to start work. There were always fires at night. We needed them for warmth, and, they said, they kept the animals away. The elephant and the thick herds of buffalo meant us no harm, but they could do a lot of damage if they trod on you in the dark.

"We are ready." Tlawi was a quiet man with sturdy legs and the thickset body of the hill people. His skin was the colour of amber, and he had the thin Hamitic lips and the high cheekbones of his forefathers who had come from the north and settled in this country many generations before.

"We are ready." They had the sacks of stakes, and the lengths of rope and the tall poles barred with red and white. Tlawi didn't carry anything. But behind him were three other men with our equipment.

When it was light enough to see we set out. We talked to the men working on the bridge, and, across the other side of the stream, to the others cutting out the road. Beyond them the lines we had pegged out the day before went up over the hill towards the dark mass of the forest. We planned to make the trace of another two days' work, and then to go on ahead and decide where to cross the next stream and where to establish our next camp.

In many parts of this District the tsetse-fly had spread so widely that there were now too many people and too many cattle in the areas that were free of it. The land they had had to leave was very badly eroded anyway. Goats and man had destroyed the trees and the bush, too many cattle had eaten too little grass, and the rain had washed the topsoil into the plains and lakes in the great rift which cut through these hills.

So instead of clearing the tsetse out of the old land we decided to try and open up new land. New land there was, rolling hills of it with good grass, and empty of man and stock: and for a very good reason. It was criss-crossed with streams which flowed from the forest which covered the tops of the hills. The vegetation which grew along the banks of these streams harboured the tsetse which cannot exist in open country. If we could thin out this vegetation without destroying the flow of the streams it would, we thought, make fine grazing land. In the end we persuaded the people we wanted to move to think so too.

I was given the job of driving a road into the area. I took about two hundred men, and tools and food for about two months. It was as I have said empty country. There was nothing to eat there except wild honey and some berries, and no people ever went there except occasionally some poachers. The poachers went there because the open grasslands, untouched by man for so long as anyone could remember, were full of game. The elephant kept for the most part to the forest, but the buffalo roamed the hills in large herds and on the lower slopes there were rhino.

It was fine, lovely country. The air was fresh and clean, and from the top of the hills where the forest began you could see for miles and miles, and there was no sign or sight of man or of his practices. The thick green forest went on and on to the edge of the Ngorogoro Crater, a dozen miles or so away, and beyond that were the wide game-filled plains of the Serengeti.

I was there for about two months. The country had never been properly charted and I used to amuse myself by marking the hills and the streams on the blank spaces and dotted lines of the old German map. I gave them names. Six months before I had been on leave in England, and searching for names I tended to use what was fresh in my mind. The short, homely English names seemed ill at ease as neighbours to the many-syllabled Masai labels that had been attached to the larger and more distant hills, but I had met a Hungarian girl with a long improbable-sounding name, and for all I know herdsmen may still point to that long, lazy valley and call it Deguidrofranck.

One day when Tlawi and I had gone on ahead to look for a site we saw a small hill with a single, windswept tree growing on it. When we reached it there was a view of a long slope curving away to the sudden wall of the rift. The wind was blowing towards us and we saw them before they saw us. The nearest were less than twenty yards away. There must have been over a hundred buffalo in the herd. Unmoving and silent, we watched them from behind a tree. I had a pair of field-glasses and Tlawi had a stick.

Suddenly Tlawi bent and picked up a stone. Before I could stop him he threw it at the bull closest to us. I had been brought up to look on buffalo as the most difficult and danger-ous of all African animals and I always treated them with the greatest respect.

The bull turned and looked at us. I turned and looked at the tree, and at the first branch twenty feet above our heads. The bull's eyes had the same smouldering purposeful look that I was to get to know many years later in bullrings in southern Spain. Then with a toss of his head he turned again and in a mo-ment the whole herd were streaming away down the valley.

"Why did you do that?" I asked.

Tlawi shrugged his shoulders.

"To see them run . . ."

Another day we were plotting the way for the road across a gully. Where the water ran under the surface it was thickly wooded and in places the sides of the gully had been steeply eroded by the rains. It wasn't easy to find a smooth crossing and we had separated to explore different routes.

Tlawi was a quiet, self-contained man and he rarely raised his voice. He was phlegmatic to a point which made the District Commissioner, himself as English as a bull-terrier, feel, as he once told me, like a temperamental opera-singer.

When he shouted at me I was therefore a little surprised. When I turned and saw him waving his arms like a demented faun I thought he must have gone out of his mind.

"Run," he was saying. "Run to the trees."

I hadn't heard anything and the snort when it came from the bushes to my left caught me by surprise. The first to appear was the baby. When he saw me he ran back into the bushes again, straight into mother.

Mother was a large one even for a rhino, which specialize in size. I ran. But I needn't have bothered. Mother wasn't in the mood for heroics either. She ran, too, much faster than I did and in the opposite direction. Behind her the baby scuttled off like an outsize piglet.

After that I carried a rifle, but it was many years before I saw another rhino.

In the evenings, after I had had my supper, I used to sit in a camp-chair by the fire and read. Sometimes I would play the gramophone which I had brought out with me. Rachmaninoff was of course a Russian, and he knew all about open empty spaces, but Beethoven was a townsman and yet his music might have been written for these empty spaces in the night. Chopin and Bach sounded a little thin here. Too urban—with too sophisticated a simplicity. They also made me feel homesick. Homesick for the fog outside the Albert Hall and for the quiet, merging colours and contours of the English countryside. But Beethoven was exactly right. The soft, hesitant bits matched the small transient circle where I sat in the light of the lamp and the fire, and the power and the violence of the tremendous crescendos were a reminder and a reflection of the untamed land and the untrodden forests which surrounded us and hemmed us in.

Best of all though was Rachmaninoff. It's rather bourgeois,

people would say even then, to like the Second Piano Concerto, and I expect they say the same now, or worse. But for me this, on a cheap portable gramophone in Africa at night, was the best that there ever was, or would be.

When the work was nearly finished I went back to headquarters to collect the money to pay the men. I can't remember what they got for a day's work, but it was very little. The ones I had with me had agreed to try and settle in this country and they were working largely for love, and their food.

When I was paying them, checking off the names on a list, I saw that one man who was marked as coming from the plain below the rift wall had the colouring and the figure of the hill people. Thinking it was a mistake I asked him.

"No," he said, "I come from there. Truly."

"But you look like a man of the hills."

"Yes," he said, "but I was a twin."

Tlawi broke in to explain. "Among our people twins are regarded as unlucky. They do not occur often with our women and so, in days past, they thought it was unnatural."

"And so . . .?" I asked.

"And so they were left out in the open to die or to be taken by a leopard. But the people of the plain did not have this custom. And gradually an arrangement was evolved. The twins were left in a certain place and the drums were sounded in a certain way, and the women of the plains, who because of fevers were often childless, came and took the twins and brought them up as their own."

When they had all been paid and we had loaded the tools and the remnants of the rations on the lorry the men walked away down the road we had made. Later another batch of men would be coming in to clear the bush along the streams.

When the lorry reached the top of the hill I told the driver to stop. I wanted to have a last look at this country. I knew that I would be going away soon and I didn't know if I would ever see it again.

From where we were we could see the line of the road showing red against the pale green of the hills. It went almost to the dark line of the forest. I tried to imagine it dotted with thatched huts and cattle and spirals of blue domestic smoke.

But I couldn't.

CHAPTER SEVENTEEN

Twenty-Seven Pellets in the Bottom

WHEN ALL the boxes and crates were packed, and the lids had been hammered in or locked, we put them in the storeroom.

"When will you be back for them?" they asked politely.

"One year. Two years—I do not know," I said. It was early in 1940 and the end of the war looked a long way away.

I put all the keys, except one which I kept and of course later lost, in an envelope and sealed it. Seven or eight years afterwards when my wife was faced with opening and sorting out this miscellany of bachelor belongings she asked where on earth I had put this famous envelope of keys. In the end we had to break all the locks, and almost at the last we found the envelope between some sheets in the tin bath. And then of course I remembered that I had put them there: but sadly, in response to another question, I couldn't remember why. It was a long time ago, I argued. But I still worry about it all the same.

I was leaving early in the morning and I said my good-byes in the evening. They were quiet amiable people with pale brown faces much marked with grooves and little furrows cut into the skin to show their tribe and clan. Some of the older men remembered the other war, but this District was in hilly country and remote so it hadn't touched them very much.

"We worked as porters for the Germans," they said. "We walked and walked but we never saw any fighting."

"Once," one of them went on, "we did see some of the English. They were riding on horses and they wore funny hats with feathers in—like we wear at our dances and ceremonies. But the Germans didn't shoot them. When we asked them why, they said it was better to save the bullets to shoot game.

"We didn't get much food in those days," he concluded with a sigh.

"Peace be on your head," they said, "and may you kill a thousand men." They drew their fingers across their throats in a delicate gesture.

I had one more thing to do before I left.

It was after dark when I got there. The lights looked friendly and warm in the cold, untenanted night. The Mission was only a dozen miles away but in this part of Africa one very quickly passed from houses and huts and fields to emptiness.

They didn't know I was coming. They had heard the sound of the car and they had been watching the lights coming up the valley. I could see from their faces that they were perplexed and worried at this unexpected call.

"How did you know?" they asked as soon as they saw who it was.

"Know what?" I said.

The Father in charge of the Mission looked at me with his shrewd yellowed eyes and tugged at his beard.

"It doesn't matter," he said. "Come in. We are pleased to see you."

When I told them I had come to say good-bye and why, they smiled.

"What good luck you have," they said, "to fight those so-and-so Boches. How we would like to go with you."

They were all Frenchmen at that Mission and they all had beards. Some were stained a little with nicotine, but they were very handsome beards.

"I go to fight the Italians actually," I said. "In Abyssinia."

One of the Fathers commented richly on that as well. I often wondered why he had become a missionary and even more how he had managed to remain one. Like Rabelais, he came from Chinon.

"We must drink a glass of wine," the Father in charge said.

They brought out half a dozen bottles of the Algerian wine they used for other purposes—and a box of cigars. There were five of us altogether. I wondered what time I should get to bed.

It wasn't until we had started on the third bottle that one of the Fathers said,

"We thought you had come about something else."

"Oh, yes?" I said. We were talking in French. Wine is a great leveller and usually more up than down.

"Yes," he said. It was my friend from Chinon. He was a large robust man with a red unascetic face.

"Well——" he went on.

The Father in charge interrupted.

"When exactly are you leaving?" he asked.

"At six in the morning," I said. "I have a long way to go."

"Ah," he said.

After a bit the man from Chinon continued with his story.

"The other day a very funny thing happened. Very droll it was. But also in a way unfortunate . . ."

It was clear that this was going to take a long time—so I gave way and lit another cigar, and they started to uncork the fourth bottle of wine.

"*Comme tu sais*," he was getting very friendly, "I have a little garden . . ."

This was a wonderful piece of understatement.

It was a bit too high and too cold in these hills for maize to grow well. But the Fathers liked their corn-on-the-cob and my friend from Chinon was a keen and knowledgeable man of the land. He had found a sheltered corner and he had sent for some special seed. He had this year, I knew, a beautiful crop of maize. It was the envy of everyone for miles around. Not least of the wild pig who lived in the forest which surrounded the Mission on three sides.

"These so-and-so pigs," he went on with adjectives that would have been a credit to Falstaff, "came into the maize night after night. I set traps—I paid men to scare them away. But it was no use . . ."

He had unbuttoned his robe and his broad much-haired chest gleamed in the hissing light of the lamps.

"So, my friend, what did I do?

"I went out myself with a gun. A twelve-bore."

Someone filled up my empty glass.

"I went out with a gun," he said it again to emphasize it. I looked at my watch. It was half-past one.

"I waited in the rows of maize. There was no moon and it

was very quiet. I heard the noise of small animals, rats and porcupines and jackals. Once I heard a leopard cough in the trees. But nothing came to the field where I was.

"And then I heard it. It was only a movement in the maize, but I knew at once that it was a pig. I crept closer and the noise stopped. 'He has heard me,' I said to myself. 'If I move any more he will go away.'

"He was, I reckoned, about thirty yards away. I only had No. 5 shot in the gun and I knew I couldn't kill him even if I hit him in the dark—but better than nothing, I thought, and as soon as I heard the noise again I fired . . .

"The scream of noise that followed was very satisfactory. At least I had hit him. But as the scream went on and on I started to wonder. It sounded less and less like a pig. I went closer and when at last I got there I found that it wasn't.

"It was a man. He was lying on the ground face down. 'Holy Mother of God,' I thought, 'I've killed him.' By this time all the huts near the field were astir and men came running out, spears and clubs in their hands.

"I called them and we carried the man to the Mission.

"He wasn't dead, but there were twenty-seven pellets in his bottom. I know. We took them out and I counted them."

He took a long draught of wine. He didn't look very sorry about it, I thought.

"Next morning," he went on, "the Father here and I went to see him. There had been a lot of blood, but we knew he wasn't badly hurt.

"I told him I thought it had been a wild pig.

"He said, 'Eh——' and clicked his tongue. He was very subdued.

" 'But you were stealing my maize . . .' I went on.

"He raised himself on his elbow and shook his head.

" 'No, Father,' he said. 'I was not stealing your maize.'

" 'Then what were you doing in my field in the middle of the night?' I asked.

" 'I was relieving myself,' he replied.

"This made me very angry.

" 'Relieving yourself in my maize? That doesn't make it any better. That is almost as bad as stealing.'

"We left him then. We didn't think we would hear any more about it. But we were wrong.

"Two days ago he came to the Mission.

" 'How is your behind?' I asked.

" 'It is better, Father,' he said.

"There was a short silence. I wondered what he wanted.

" 'Do you want work?' I asked.

" 'No, Father.'

" 'Then what is it?' I was getting irritable.

" 'I want my money.'

" 'What money?'

" 'The money for my wound. The compensation.'

"So that was it, I said to myself. I talked the matter over with the Father here and in the end we paid him some money. And he went away.

"But this evening just before nightfall he came again.

" 'It is not enough,' he said.

" 'What do you want?' I asked.

" 'I want five shillings for every pellet.' He produced a crumpled piece of paper.

" 'In all a hundred and thirty-five shillings.'

"This was too much. We told him to go to the devil.

"As he went down the steps he turned and said, 'I will go to the D.C. He will make you pay.'

"And half an hour later you came."

He slapped his leg and bellowed with laughter.

"*Mon Dieu*, we were scared. And now at six in the morning you go off to the war. Life is very droll . . ."

I didn't get off at six the next morning, but by seven o'clock I was driving along the dusty earth road towards the north. I wasn't feeling at all like going to war. My mouth was dry and my head ached.

But when I reached the crest of the hill I felt better. A cool morning wind came down from the wooded hills on my left and below me the plain was spread out in wave after wave of green like a sea. Herds of zebra and impala, dots of black and white and brown, were feeding on the grass and above me some vultures were circling against the hard clear blue of the sky.

I wondered when I would see this sort of country again: and as I started on down the long winding hill I wondered too how they would assess the twenty-seven pellets in the Missionaries' field of maize.

And just for once I was glad that I wouldn't be there.

CHAPTER EIGHTEEN

The War

I ARRIVED in Nairobi to join the Army at half-past five. I went straight to the place where I had been told to report, but it was shut. A notice said, "Hours 9 to 12, and 2 to 5."

This was my first surprise about the Army. I didn't expect it to shut down at five o'clock. I thought somehow that they went on all the time. But eventually I got myself entered on a form and equipped with the basic implements of war. I spent much of my time in Nairobi in a room at Torr's learning where to start winding my puttees so that they finished in the right place.

I wasn't really a great success as a private soldier so they sent me to an O.C.T.U. Here my university education enabled me to talk and drink my way through the instructors and to everyone's surprise I finished up with the Sword of Honour. There weren't any swords actually as they had been called in for scrap, but they gave me a cheque so that later I could have my revolver suitably inscribed.

The Battle of Britain was on then, and the Italians were massing like vultures on their side of the border, listening to the news about the Germans and hoping very much that it would soon enable them to march into Kenya in unopposed splendour. So we all went off on a week's leave feeling that it was likely to be our last. The cheque came in very useful.

Instead of going off to the front like a sacrificial lamb as I expected, I was sent to help with a new battalion of the King's African Rifles which was being formed in Tanganyika. I felt rather a fraud going back there again but in the end we worked our way up to Abyssinia. I stayed with this Battalion until the end of what is called the Abyssinian campaign, and then I went on to the Brigade staff. The Brigade stayed on in Addis Ababa until the middle of 1942 as a sort of rearguard until most of the Italians had been removed and the Emperor Haile Selassie was firmly in the saddle again, and it then started on a series of moves which took it eventually to Burma.

The next three chapters are about Abyssinia. There is not very much about fighting in them because, like a lot of other people during the war, we spent most of the time doing other and much less bellicose things. There was an air of dry-mouthed unreality about the whole of my time in that lovely and enchanting country. It was largely no doubt a question of altitude, because we were mostly at six or eight or even ten thousand feet above sea-level. But even in the flat ugly parts it was peculiar. Some people said this was due to the heat which was usually well into the hundreds, but I am inclined to think it was due as much to some splendid savages called the Danakil, who hovered around us eyeing our private parts with a predatory eye and a sharp knife. They were very pleasant about it on the rare occasions when, well supported, we met them. "It's one of our little customs," they would explain, but we all found it rather disturbing. We soon adopted the practice of other peoples who dealt with the Danakil and conducted our negotiations with them through Somali ladies borrowed for the occasion, and well briefed.

CHAPTER NINETEEN

When the Askari went to War

ASKARI is the word they use in East Africa for a soldier. Large numbers of Africans were put into uniform during the war. Not all of them were issued with rifles and fought the enemy, but a great many did. To start with the enemy was the Italians and the fighting was not always either severe or protracted. Later many of them went to Burma where the enemy was the Japanese. There the fighting was always tough, and sometimes it was terrible.

People learn quickly in wartime and they see and experience things that would otherwise never have come their way. It is a great forcing house, and the more unsophisticated, untravelled and inexperienced a person is the more dramatic and impressive the process becomes. The war made a great impact on the East African Askari.

Once I was out for a walk and I came across a group of men under a tree. They hadn't seen me coming and I heard what they were saying. One soldier, a corporal from a tribe I knew, was teaching the others English.

"When you are pleased," he was explaining, "you say 'Good show.'" The corporal had worked before the war as a schoolmaster in a Government school run on public-school lines for the sons of chiefs.

"And when you are not pleased?" someone asked.

"When you are not pleased you say 'Bloody fool.' "

I stayed with them for some time.

"Yes," they said. "We all want to learn English. It is the key."

"The key?" I asked.

"Yes, Bwana. It is the key to the future. When we go back to our villages and our towns after the war we don't want to go back to the past. We want to go back to the future. But we must have the key to it ready in our hands. Otherwise the opportunity will slip away."

"Hasn't the spreading of Swahili as a form of common language all over East Africa been another sort of key?" I asked.

"Yes," they said, "but it is only a little key. It is true that it has made it possible for Africans to speak to one another where without it they could not have done. We would have remained locked behind the prison of our own tribal tongues."

"It has also," said one of the Askari, "enabled us to speak to Europeans and Indians and Arabs, and they to us. And that is good."

One of the soldiers was a Kikuyu from Kenya. He hadn't said anything up till then but when he started to speak he held the stage like a practised orator and gestured gracefully and a little theatrically with his hands.

"In Kenya," he said, "it would have been better had Swahili never come. In your country," the sweep of his hand embraced the others and the corporal and me who came from Tanganyika, "the people, both the Europeans and the Africans, have had the good fortune or the application to learn Swahili properly and through it they can understand one another. In this way it has become a link and a bond between men of different colour and different tribes.

"But in Kenya," he went on, "it has not been the same. Neither the Europeans nor the Africans have a tradition of speaking good Swahili. Indeed they have, the one and the other, taken a pride in speaking it badly, as if to speak it well was a sin.

"The result is that except for a few Europeans who have taken the trouble to learn the tribal languages, and the few Africans who have learnt to speak English, there has never been any understanding between them. When an English farmer tells his servant to bring the whisky and to hoe a field the language he uses which they call Ki-settler is sufficient. It is understood. But when a farmer wants to explain something complicated, or when a Kikuyu wants to explain the real reasons for doing something and for not doing something to his master they have no language in common.

"And out of this grows misunderstanding, and out of mis-understanding grow anger and hate, and fear and revenge."

After that no one said anything for some time.

One thing that surprised the Askari in Abyssinia were the girls. In most African tribal societies standards of morality are as high as in, for example, Latin countries, and the sanctions for breaches of these standards are harsh and sometimes cruel. In the towns, of course, and on sisal estates, manned by immigrant labour from different places and, some say, on Mission stations too, the old sanctions and standards have sometimes eroded or disappeared, as they have done in other places.

The willingness, indeed the eagerness of the girls, even in the Muslim parts of Abyssinia, to be friendly bemused the

Askari at first. They started by being suspicious, as they were apt to be of anything new, but when they found the friendliness was warm and, what's more, that it was usually free as well, they overcame their suspicions and co-operated with zest.

This, of course, had its complications. Later when they went to Ceylon and India and Burma they used to wander round the villages, smiling at the girls, and knocking on doors as they had done with impunity, and more, in Abyssinia. It took us some time to persuade them that things had changed, and even longer to persuade the local people to understand the reasons for it.

A more immediate problem was V.D. I don't know what the statistics were but one had the impression that the V.D. figures in the towns in Abyssinia must have been astronomical. Quite apart from anything else we had to keep the Askari fit to fight when the occasion arose and to have half the strength of a Battalion in hospital or on light duty didn't look very good in the monthly returns.

So I started a brothel. All the girls were, to put it mildly, volunteers, and there was no difficulty at all in finding recruits.

I used to inspect it on Thursdays, and the M.O. went there on Tuesdays and Fridays. It was run on the best public-school lines, and there were prefects and houses and in a manner of speaking there were house colours as well. It had been equipped at the outset with written rules and in the short time it lived it developed both a tradition and a specialized vocabulary. This had a definite Etonian bias through a subaltern who helped me in the venture. The girls who qualified for Pop quickly became an aristocracy, plus five per cent.

When we had reduced the V.D. rate among the troops from 35 to 8 per cent the authorities in Nairobi, to whom copies of our Battalion reports were apparently sent, got suspicious.

Enquiries were made and we were told to close the place down.

It was a pity, I thought, and so did the Askari and so did the girls. However, for six months Bates's brothel was among the best-kept secrets of the war.

During the war the African and the European, living at closer quarters together than had usually happened before, got to learn a lot about one another. Much of it was new to both of them and sometimes it was very surprising. The sight of thousands upon thousands of Italians in the humility and subjection of quickly improvised prisoner-of-war camps inevitably made the African lose something of the awe with which he had often regarded the possessor of a white skin. And later the poverty and squalor and hunger he saw in India and in Burma radically altered his attitude when he returned to the Indian trader in his village shop and the Sikh carpenter at the bench next to his.

Generally, however, I believe the closer contact and the greater knowledge did much good to both sides. In it were laid the seeds of the racial harmony which has surprised many people when they read of developments in Tanganyika since the war, and the beginnings of the ideas and the ideals behind the multi-racial groups and parties that have been formed in Kenya in recent years. It is no coincidence I think that one of the best and most respected of the Battalion commanders in East Africa was Lt.-Colonel Michael Blundell.

CHAPTER TWENTY

Iodine

I RANG up after breakfast about the inspection.
Iodine was very angry.

"Twenty-four hours' notice is the absolute minimum."

"I'm sorry, Iodine—but it's the Brigadier."

"The Brigadier? That makes it even worse. For a Brigadier
I need at least thirty-six hours.

"For a General," he added, "I'd want a week."

"One more thing," I persisted, hating myself. "You'll have
to wear boots."

The reply was a silence at the other end of the field telephone which could be heard in every corner of the Orderly Room.

"Boots? Don't be ridiculous. You know I can't wear boots."

"I'm sorry, but you'll have to. The Brigadier . . ."

After the Brigadier had been consigned to a place rarely visited by Regular soldiers, Iodine became reasonable. This didn't happen often but when it did it was very dangerous.

"Now listen, old boy," he began.

In the end I promised to speak to the C.O. The outcome was that Iodine could wear his tennis-shoes, but they must be clean.

The inspection was at half-past three.

We watched the dust of the Brigadier's car approaching across the plain. Over the hills a few vultures were hovering. The fighting had ended a week ago, but vultures had good memories. The odds were, I thought, that Iodine was watching the vultures. He was very keen on birds and a Brigadier's inspection wouldn't prevent him putting first things first.

When we were approaching B Company the Brigadier asked who the Company Commander was.

The C.O. looked at me. "You'd better explain."

"Well, sir . . ." It wasn't easy. Iodine didn't fit into any sort of category. He was a Game Ranger in Tanganyika. "He knows a lot about elephant and snakes." It didn't sound very convincing, so I added, "He's a wonderful shot."

The Brigadier nodded.

Encouraged, I told him where Iodine had been at school.

"At Rugby? How interesting," said the Brigadier.

It was quite easy once you got the hang of it.

"And he is a bachelor, sir . . ." the summary concluded. "Very much so." That was meant as a touch of humour, but the Brigadier didn't smile and he was beginning to look a bit suspicious. The C.O. thought he had better intervene.

"He's a bit unorthodox, sir, but he's really jolly good. The trouble is his feet . . ."

"His feet?"

"Well, he can walk for miles but they are . . . Anyway, he can't wear boots."

The Brigadier let this pass. "Let's go and look at them then."

When they came into sight we could see some visual signalling going on. By the time we arrived at Company H.Q. Iodine had climbed down from the roof and had put his field-glasses away.

I was sweating under the armpits but everything looked all right. They might have been inspecting an ordinary Company.

The Brigadier was very impressed with Iodine. He knew the name of every Askari, his tribe and where he came from. He even remembered the names of all his officers. He seemed to know every inch of the country around. The birds were good in most parts of Abyssinia and here they were very good.

"Now let's see some Company drill."

The Brigadier was in a very jovial mood.

"Right, sir." Iodine seemed to have the situation in hand. I had warned him of course that this would probably be on the menu but I wasn't very happy about it.

It wasn't easy to follow Iodine's words of command but the troops seemed to understand and they put up a very good show. Once I caught Iodine's eye, and received in reply a wink and a wolfish grin.

"Pretty good," said the Brigadier. "Now form them up over there in two lines facing east."

I saw Iodine's face. I looked away and then backed as far from the Brigadier as I could without making it too obvious.

Iodine faced his Company. He brought them to attention.

The word of command reverberated across the plain, but the last note was strained. It was cleverly done. Iodine opened his mouth for the next order but no sound came from it. He tried again. Then he turned smartly and marched to the Brigadier.

"I'm sorry, sir. My voice has gone. With your permission my second-in-command will carry on."

On the way to the Company office we passed a long green hut. It looked in excellent condition but all the windows were shuttered and the doors were locked.

"What's that?" The Brigadier may have been the only one there who didn't know that Iodine couldn't, without careful rehearsal, move a platoon fifteen yards except at the gallop, but little else escaped him.

"It's shut, I'm afraid, sir," said Iodine without batting an eyelid. "The people before had a mild case of leprosy in there so I thought I'd better close it up."

The Brigadier hesitated but in the end we walked on. On one side of the Company office there was a door marked MAP ROOM. It looked very efficient.

Iodine tried very hard to keep the Brigadier away from it but in the end he had to open the door.

For a naturalist it was really most interesting. The wing of the Lammergeyer, pinned to the table for setting, wasn't something you see every day and the skin of the Yellow-bellied Eremomela was a collector's item. In a box there were half a dozen young striped sand-snakes. In one corner were several maps, rolled up. One of them had recently been used to stun a troublesome owl and looked as if it had been through several arduous campaigns.

The Brigadier took this very well, considering.

This surely must be the end, I thought, as they stood on the wooden steps. It was nearly six o'clock and I felt unusually thirsty. But the inspection wasn't quite over.

Along the track which led to the village half a mile away two figures in white were approaching. The pace was leisurely but assured. They had clearly walked this road many times before. As they passed the office they gave a polite salute to Iodine. He didn't return it, and the girls continued unabashed on their way. They paused outside the door of the green hut, and one of them pulled out a key from the depths of her Abyssinian robe and unlocked it.

"And who might they be?" asked the Brigadier.

"Oh, they are probably bringing eggs to sell or something." The "sir" came afterwards on a somewhat lower note.

"But I thought . . ." said the Brigadier.

"Well, sir, as a matter of fact we do use one end as a . . . as a kind of club."

"A club? Troops' welfare?" One could see the Brigadier was very interested.

"Yes, sir . . . sort of . . ."

There was a long pause. Then the Brigadier said, "I see."

On the way back to the Battalion H.Q. he broke another long silence.

"Does the M.O. see them?"

The C.O. looked the Brigadier in the eye and said,

"Yes, sir. Once a week. Regularly."

Soon afterwards the Brigadier was promoted. He had been a very understanding Brigadier, and we were all very pleased. Later on he came from Division to inspect us again. The signal he sent ended: "No need for Iodine to wear boots, but Troops' Welfare is out."

CHAPTER TWENTY-ONE

The Battle of Gondar

At about one o'clock in the morning we got out of the lorries and started to walk. We were all glad of the change. The top of the pass was over ten thousand feet up and it was very cold. Apart from that the lorries had been driving up the escarpment without lights and even in the dark it was better not to look at the drop over the edge.

On our way we passed columns of the battalion we were relieving. We exchanged rude remarks in a hushed, apprehensive whisper. It was the first time for us and we were wondering what we would think about it. When we reached the cross-roads I remembered that it was my birthday.

The shells started to come over while we were having breakfast. The first one went off with a nasty metallic splash, but the next three just made a dull thud. In the course of the two weeks

H   113

or so that we were there we worked out that on an average one Italian shell in five went off. We wondered what the girls working in the factories in Turin would have thought of that; or of the fact that the total damage done by the one thousand three hundred-odd shells they fired at us was two black eyes and a stray dog.

By the end of breakfast we were sufficiently reassured to be plotting the fall of the shells on the other companies with a certain amount of glee. There is no doubt that war makes even the most ordinary civilians a bit peculiar.

Iodine rang up on the field telephone soon afterwards.

"These bloody shells are disturbing the birds." He wanted someone to go in straight away and spike the guns and the gunners with the bayonet.

"My chaps are busy," he explained. Probably rigging up bird-tables, the C.O. thought.

This was the last stronghold of the Italians in Abyssinia. They were holding a town called Gondar under an unusually tough and tenacious commander. We were dotted about on a long mound of hill and across a valley the Italians were well dug in on the slope of another hill.

At about eleven o'clock we had our first real taste of war. It came from the air. From Wellington bombers of the Royal Air Force actually. This time all the bombs went off. We screamed down the field telephone to Brigade, and Brigade no doubt screamed down the telephone to someone else. We found it awfully difficult to explain this little mistake to the African soldiery. Fortunately it didn't happen again. The R.A.F., we found, were very good aimers.

Just before we took over this position a rather unusual thing had happened. A small detachment of Free French arrived one afternoon and announced that they had been attached to us for the battle. We found out that this was true. Brigade H.Q. had forgotten to tell us in the rush of events. They were an engaging collection of ex-taxi-drivers and bistro-keepers from Marseilles and Perpignan and they were very tough and self-contained. There was also a Senegalese named Marie-Joseph and he, it turned out, was the only officer among them. He was a splendid chap and much respected by the taxi-drivers and bistro-keepers, but to start with, at any rate, our Askari were a little surprised. As far as I remember the only African officer in the King's African Rifles then was the present Kabaka of Uganda and he, I think, was a quartermaster. Our C.O. was also a little surprised but in the end he got very attached to them and would tell Marie-Joseph long stories in English, of which Marie-Joseph knew only three not very nice words, about the North-West Frontier.

"And there they were," he would say, "those damned wogs —oh, sorry, old chap . . ."

Marie-Joseph used to ask me afterwards what the stories were about.

Our Free French assortment had only a loose sort of attachment to us, and they always preferred to work on their own. Marie-Joseph would come into the orderly room and say that during the night they would be going off over there. He would point vaguely in the direction so that we wouldn't fire on them when they came back. What time? He didn't know really. About what time? "*Ça dépend*," he would always reply, with a wolfish grin.

They didn't take any guns with them. They just carried knives and short business-like-looking pieces of rope. "Guns weigh so much," they said. "Very fatiguing." Marie-Joseph, however, always took a tommy-gun. "In case your soldiers molest us when we return," he explained.

It was they who told us that some of the Italians kept a supply of local girls in their dug-outs. Often the Frenchmen would be away for several days.

A few days before the final assault on the Italian positions was launched the 25-pounders behind us started shelling the enemy hills at night. Our C.O. was a keen bridge player and we used to play with him in the evenings after supper. Up to then it had usually been fairly quiet at night, but when the 25-pounders started they made so much noise we could hardly hear ourselves call. Whenever I play bridge now, which isn't often, I think about those evenings and how easy it was to revoke when you heard the slow revolving song of the shells as they went up over our heads, to land later with a satisfying scrunch on the Italians and their girls in the trenches opposite.

The unpleasant part of the assault didn't last very long and the trouble came more from landmines than from any shooting. When we reached the other side the Italians very sensibly got out their white flags and called it a day. They seemed very well equipped in this respect and when we looked at the flags after-wards we found that they were mass-produced articles and one got the impression that they were standard army equipment. Flags, white, for surrender.

The soldiers, and most of the officers, seemed very relieved that it was all over and most of them came out with their hands up and their suitcases ready-packed at their feet.

The Brigadier, who had a nice sense of theatre, rode into Gondar at the head of his troops on a donkey. It was a rather moth-eaten donkey but it was the best we could do at short notice. The Brigadier was a large, well-fleshed man and one could tell that the donkey didn't think much of the war. Even when you beat him he only blinked his eyes. He was clearly a pacifist and he wasn't, it seemed, the only one.

CHAPTER TWENTY-TWO

The Missing Ear

THE shop was halfway up the hill, on the left. One of the windows displayed furs and skins, and things made out of them like handbags and tippets. Some of the watch-straps looked slightly human. In 1942 almost anything could happen in Addis Ababa.

The other window was always shuttered.

We, like everyone else in Addis, were always losing things. Tinned sardines and cartridges were fairly easy both to write off and to replace, but complete lorry engines and bottles of whisky were more difficult. Once we lost a 15-hundredweight truck, a battleship-scraper and a Staff Captain all in one night. The battleship-scraper had arrived unexpectedly a month before in an enormous truck and we were really rather relieved when it disappeared.

There were suggestions that some of these missing things found their way to the shop up the hill. This at any rate was what I told the Brigadier. I was curious to see what was inside.

"All right, then," he said. "You'd better go and have a dekko."

It was very gloomy and musty inside. No one seemed to be about.

The voice when it came arrived from the roof.

"Welcome." He spoke in English but the tone was very melodramatic. Later, and in his own good time, he added in a slow, measured bass, "I have not seen you before." I shivered a little in the gloom.

Above me overlapping the gallery that ran along one side of the room was a beard. Black and ragged and tangled. Rather like the last month's mess accounts, I thought. I was already a little light-headed.

Slowly the beard came down the stairs.

"And what, my friend, is your pleasure?"

He spoke quite good English really, but it sounded like something else.

"Well," I said, "I'd like to look round if I may. I want something for my wife . . ."

I had rehearsed this beforehand but it didn't sound very convincing in the rarefied atmosphere of the shop. Things weren't improved by an enormous blow on the shoulder nor by the burst of laughter which came afterwards.

"Your wife? Ha!" He lowered his voice. "Do you know, my friend? I do not think you have a wife."

I hadn't actually, but how on earth did he know? Caught off-balance I conceded the point too quickly.

"Well, for someone, you know . . ." I said. This wasn't my Inspector Carstairs manner at all.

Having won the first round on points he relaxed a bit.

"My name is Arogov," he explained. "I am a Russian—a White Russian. I am also a Grand Duke." It was said without pride.

I noticed that a piece of his right ear was missing. Quite a large piece.

We went round the shop. There seemed to be nothing but skins and furs. But I did see a pile of army greatcoats on the floor. He dismissed these with a wave of his hand.

"Italian. I bought them from a Colonel. Unfortunately you people arrived before I was able to pay him." He shrugged sadly. "*C'est la guerre.*

"For your friend now," he went on. I waited for another blow on the shoulder but the wink that came instead hurt even more. "Something like this."

He opened a drawer. The thing inside was not really suitable for any kind of friend.

"Mistake," he said.

The next drawer was full of filigree work. I bought a couple of bracelets for the record.

It was all very disappointing. He had several unusual things in other drawers and cupboards, but there was clearly nothing here that had ever belonged to the British Army.

As I was leaving he said, "I have some Armenian arak. Let us have a little drink."

He had learned his English, he told me, in Jibuti.

"For a time," he explained, "I used to work the gramophone in a little establishment there. One of the ladies on the staff was English and she taught me in the mornings. It was not a very good job for a Grand Duke, I know, but there were—what do you say?—hidden emoluments."

He must have seen me looking at his ear. He touched it.

"That was the same lady, *la petite anglaise*. She was not very phlegmatic, that one."

He opened his mouth and then shut his teeth with a snap. He was a very laconic Russian.

I often used to go there after that. I got to like Arogov very much.

Some months afterwards the time came for us to leave Addis Ababa. It was on a Thursday that I paid my last visit to the shop.

"Ah, it is sad," he said when I told him. "Before you go I would like you to come to my house. Please."

He took me to a part of the town I had not been to before. We went in his car. "Italian," he said as he hooted his way through the crowds. It certainly looked rather Latin, but the sound of the engine was, I thought, familiar. Like a British Army 15-hundredweight truck.

His family was very nice. I wasn't quite sure which exactly of the three ladies was his wife, but the children were enchanting.

I had noticed the large shed in the backyard when we had arrived but the doors were shut. When it was time for me to go and we were on our way to the car the door of the shed was open. A large diesel truck was there, loading up. Tyres and back axles they were mostly, but there were a few cases of Australian whisky and Gordon's gin.

"Interesting, no?" he said. He didn't seem at all nonplussed. Almost everything except the missing Staff Captain seemed to be there.

As he drove me back through the twisting streets he took both hands off the wheel and clapped me on the back.

"You look worried, my friend."

I didn't know what to say. I doubted in any case whether I could find my way again to his home, and after all in a few days we would be miles away.

But I couldn't leave the question mark curled up inside me.

"All those things?" I asked. "Where do they come from?"

"From *les braves Anglais*. Where else?"

"But . . ." I began.

"But," he countered, "do not worry. Do not worry. I bought them from a General."

I didn't like to ask what sort of General he meant. There had been so many of them from so many different countries in Abyssinia in the last few years. But I've often wondered which one it was.

CHAPTER TWENTY-THREE

Lunch Party

THERE was always a smell of blue gums and donkey-dung in the town. Even in the long, low room on the top of the hill where I was playing backgammon with the Brigadier, it seeped in through the window, and competed with whiffs of bully-beef and baked beans, which came from the kitchen.

When the telephone rang I got up and answered it.

"Ah! My good friend." The voice was faint but familiar. This particular line was not very good.

"...invite you to luncheon..." was all I got of the next bit.

"Where?" I shouted.

"At the Palace. The old Palace."

This, I thought, must be a new place. One of the daytime night clubs perhaps which were beginning to spring up as the war receded.

". . . about three hundred . . ." the voice continued.

I was getting more and more foxed as the crackling in the line swallowed up larger and larger chunks of the conversation.

"All right," I said in the end. "I'll come round this evening and talk about it."

"And who in the devil was that?" The Brigadier obviously wanted to get on with the backgammon. He was winning.

The A.D.C. had been for a few eventful terms at a private school in Cornwall, where they had said the climate was better for people from abroad, and he spoke good English. He also smoked a pipe, but it obviously wasn't Barney's.

"Yes," he said. "His Highness would like to ask you to luncheon." He listened to the B.B.C. and always frowned a little when I talked about lunch.

"On Tuesday," he went on, "at one o'clock."

"His Highness wishes to be democratic. He would like three hundred guests. All the officers, and the rest . . .

"There will be five courses," he added.

I could see that this was going to be difficult. Tuesday was only two days away: and there were only about thirty officers left. The rest, apart from a few Rhodesian N.C.O.s, were very fine soldiers in swamps and jungle, but they weren't exactly knife-and-fork men. To prepare them for a five-course banquet was going to call for some intensive training.

"This is all terribly kind . . ." I began.

"Yes," he said, "let us go and have a pint at the Lion and Leopard."

He had, I found out later, a slight interest in the Lion and Leopard. He had invented the name himself. It wasn't actually very like an English pub, but he was certainly trying to make me feel at home.

"Wouldn't it be better," I tried again, "if instead of asking us all to a five-course lunch His Highness sent the soldiers some oxen to roast and some local beer to swill? They would, I think, be much happier and just as grateful."

"No doubt," said the A.D.C., "but the matter has already been decided. Do you like the barmaid? Her name is Dawn."

She looked very past sunset to me but I nodded politely: and we had another pint of beer. It wasn't actually beer, but it was served in tankards.

In the end I gave up arguing. When I got back the Brigadier wasn't very pleased about it.

Tuesday was a fine, clear morning. It didn't start to rain until twenty past twelve. By the time the troops disembarked from the three-ton lorries at five to one the sun had come out again. The steam rising from two hundred and seventy evaporating soldiers made a pretty sight in the open air as they marched into the banqueting hall. Inside visibility quickly became poor.

His Highness took his seat at a quarter to two. The Brigadier wasn't very pleased about this either. Apparently some rather complicated local version of summer time had been introduced. I wished very much that I had gone into the Navy.

Most of the guests, however, didn't mind the wait at all. There was plenty to see and touch that was quite new to them. To start with there was the cutlery: knives and forks and spoons were examined, fingered, smelt and tested for sharpness. There were tumblers and wineglasses that were much better than the tin mugs issued by the quartermaster, and they also made a pleasant tinkle when they were dropped on the floor. The napkins could be wound round the head to make even the sergeants look like girls, and the salt-cellars were very refreshing to suck.

I was very glad when the soup arrived. For a time the room sounded like the contented gurgle of a Devon trout-stream.

The A.D.C. had had to raise a rather scratch team of waiters and girls to serve a meal on this scale, and some of the girls gave the impression of being more experienced at other occupations. Some odd, and a few rather unfortunate, things began to happen. The fish, for example, which was next on the menu, came in attended by a large family of cats, and it wasn't only the cats that got fed with titbits and stroked. Some of us got the meat and even the fruit before the fish, and some people I saw got them all together on the same plate.

"They are enjoying themselves," my neighbour said, in what sounded like Upper Cantonese, but was actually Middle East French. He was one of our hosts. "See how they like the chickens." He sounded rather regretful. At our table we had waiters.

With one thing and another it was getting hot in the banqueting hall. It was a thirst-making heat. The service on this score was good, and one only had to sip one's glass for it to be filled to the brim. There was plenty to drink and some variety, and sometimes, of course, the waiters made mistakes and topped up imported Australian beer with Algerian wine, and vice versa. The soldiers, it seemed, got even better service than we did, but it was mostly a local brew made, I was told, from rice and discarded bicycle tyres.

It was heady stuff. I hoped the party wouldn't go on too long.

At about half past three the ice-cream arrived. The troops treated it with great respect at first but one by one they laid down the silly little spoons and used the more efficient implements which God had given them. By this time we were all perspiring freely, and the dark, happy faces became streaked with white (it was vanilla ice-cream) as hands were switched from one operation to another. One enormous corporal, whom I knew particularly well, raised his head from the dish when he had licked it clean and grinned with a face that was shining white from ears to eyebrows.

The ice-cream was undoubtedly a great success, but it was clearly time to go. Even the waiters and the serving girls were huddled in corners, limp, bruised and exhausted.

I looked at the main table where His Highness, poker-faced and anxious, was sipping a glass of orange squash. The Brigadier was rather red in the face. I saw him lean across and in a moment they rose and it was all over.

Outside in the bare courtyard there were some flowering shrubs. They weren't much cover for three hundred men but they were better than nothing. But it was unlikely, I thought, as later I watched the three-ton lorries drive away, that they would ever flower again.

CHAPTER TWENTY-FOUR

The Pare

IN 1944 I was released from the Army to go back to Tanganyika. We were in the Far East then but most of the time I had been in Abyssinia.

I was posted to a District in the northern part of the country. I was only there for six months to start with, but later I went back again and it was the first District of which I myself had charge. For convenience I have lumped these two periods together.

As District Commissioner I tended to spend more time on what was really the core of our job in Africa. Under the somewhat cynical and rather nineteenth-century title of Indirect Rule, the Government recognized, and if need be sought out and re-established, the traditional tribal chiefs and councils, and it was up to us to support and develop them as an integral part of the machinery of administration. Sometimes they needed restraining and sometimes they needed prodding. One pushed sometimes, usually but not always gently, from behind, or one dangled a carrot in front.

In the latter stages they had imposed on them the outward trappings of democracy. Elections and budgets and assemblies, and so on. I say 'trappings' because most tribal organizations contained, and had for generations contained, democratic checks and balances of their own not unlike those painfully and slowly extracted by the people of England from their own kings and queens. But a new element was emerging in Africa largely as a result of education and of opportunities created by the Government and by the Missions. There were teachers and clerks and shopkeepers, and many others ranging from graduates of British universities to those of both sexes who had just learnt the heady and exciting crafts of reading and writing at village schools. Provision clearly had to be made for them, both as a matter of right and as a matter of practical necessity if the traditional rulers and systems were to cope with these new elements and to survive the impact of town-bred nationalism. But it was often unpopular and always suspect to start with both by the Chiefs who were to be constrained and even by those for whose benefit it was introduced.

Not all these stories are about such fascinating and serious matters, but they are all set in the Pare District where of all the places in Africa that I knew the people were I think the most intelligent, the most likeable and the most capable of ordering their own affairs. I only hope they will forgive me.

CHAPTER TWENTY-FIVE

The Rain-maker

SOON after I arrived there was a crisis.

The messenger with his khaki tunic and his infinitely creased copper-coloured skin hinted with a half-smile that this was something unusual, something that might perplex the Bwana.

"There are some women to see you, sir," he said.

"About what?" I asked.

"About rain."

It was three o'clock in the afternoon. The sun shone with a dry, consuming harshness in a hard, metallic sky. Swirls of dust made the thin brittle leaves of the maize stir with a sound like the arid rubbings of grasshoppers.

"Well, bring them in," I said.

Another half-smile. "There are many."

"How many?"

"About fifty. Some of the women," he added unnecessarily, "are very large."

We both looked round my small office. "All right," I said. "Tell them to wait for me under the mango tree."

It was some time before the spokeswoman revealed herself. At last, after a protracted show of diffidence and unwillingness, she uncoiled herself from her base. She adjusted the folds of the red and blue patterned cloth which was wound round her body and spat economically in the dust.

"Bwana," she started, "we are the women of this valley. We are working women who till the fields and plant the crops."

"Eh . . ." an undercurrent of chorus gave approval to this opening gambit.

"Every year, generation after generation, as the time for the rain approaches we have taken gifts to Alani the rain-maker—and to his father, and his father's father before him."

"Ah . . ." a sorrowful repentant chorus encouraged her.

"This year we did not do so."

By a single step towards me she isolated herself from the group of women. She was tall and angular with a smooth harsh face and a quiet controlled voice. She had lost her looks but her body was straight and supple.

"This year we did not do so." She repeated it, and the crowd of women became watchful and silent. "Some women said it was a foolish and pagan thing to do. Some women said the gifts of money and of beer and of goats were a waste. Some women said Alani was a fraud." There was infinite scorn in her voice. Each withering arrow of comment was clearly aimed at groups of women within the group. Each seemed to find its mark. The young girls, with their European frocks and gilt Mission crosses, examined their toes and picked their noses.

The gaunt, poker-faced grandmothers scowled and muttered among themselves.

"When the first rains came we planted. Since then there has been no rain. The sky is cloudless, the wind is from the north. Soon the young maize plants will wither and die, and then what shall we, and our menfolk and the children, eat?"

I knew what they would eat but I said nothing. I had dealt with the complications of Government famine relief before. I waited.

The spokeswoman sat down. Her part had been played. From the back of the crowd another woman rose. This time it was one of the gaunt poker-faced grandmothers. "Now we want Alani the rain-maker to help us. A few days ago some of us made the journey to see him. We took the customary gifts. We asked his pardon. He abused us. We asked for his help. He refused us."

There was a pause. At last it came: "Only you can help us. Help us, Bwana."

Just before dawn I set off for the hills. With me went two goats, a thirsty-looking porter with a huge calabash full of local beer, and in my pocket fifty shillings in crumpled notes.

In five hours' walking we did not meet another person. The track wound up zigzag through the forest, and then, out in the waves and rollers of the open grasslands, it followed the economical, easy lines of elephant migrations. In the early morning a leopard coughed warily in the undergrowth: in the open hills a herd of buffalo scented us almost before we sighted them browsing across a valley, turned like ordered troops and streamed out of sight.

Alani lived in a clearing set in a clump of bush which clung to the triangle above a small valley. From a long way off we had seen the blue shifting smoke of his fire and heard his dogs barking. When we came into the clearing his sons and their sons were grouped round the fire, waiting, although I had not known myself twelve hours before that I would come to this place farther down the valley. I sent the gifts, the beer and the goats wordlessly with a messenger. There must be no unseemly hurry, and it wasn't until I had washed and eaten and smoked a pipe that I made my way along to the huts above.

Alani was a very old man, but he slowly stood up uncreaking and erect when I inquired for him. I motioned him to sit and for a while we faced one another waiting for the other to speak. He wore a rough cap of impala skin on his head, and over his shoulders, furrowed and shiny with age, he wore a thin thread-bare blanket. A clean white cloth was wound round his waist and his feet were bare. Only the toes scuffling the earth moved. His face, and his hands, were in quiet and absolute repose.

In the end I said: "I have come for your help. Down in the valley there is no rain. The crops that were planted in hope with the first small rain are dying. The women are ashamed to come to you because they did not follow the custom of their mothers and their grandmothers and seek your help in the beginning."

The old man spat on the ground and cleared his throat. His voice was frail and brittle and he was angry. "Why should I help them, Bwana? Why? They have rejected me."

"They are sorry now," I said.

In one of the huts behind us a child was crying. It was a brief, hungry cry and it was quickly stilled. I went on: "If some of the women in the valley who are too fat and too contented should go hungry I will not weep. But I do not like to see children round-bellied and thin-legged with lack of food."

Round the old man's neck was a piece of string. Suspended

from it was a small bag, made like his cap from impala skin. He drew the string over his head and opened the neck of the bag. With the back of his hand he smoothed the dry, dusty earth and then spilled the contents on the ground. The largest object was the desiccated carcass of a locust. There were several pieces of bone, and the seeds of plants and grasses. There were strands of hair and pieces of resin from the barks of trees. There were a number of other things that I could not identify.

For perhaps five minutes he concentrated on these objects. Occasionally he would turn one over with his little finger. Suddenly he scooped the objects up and put them back into the bag. "Very well, Bwana. I will try. I will pray to God for rain."

To me this was something of an anti-climax. I don't know quite what I had expected but it certainly was not this quiet humility. I got up. When I thanked him he said: "I want you to know I am not doing this to help the people of the valley. They have rejected me, and I do not care if the children cry from hunger."

In the evening I sent word to Alani and asked him to come and talk to me. It was cold in the hills at night and we sat round a brushwood fire. Eventually I asked him: "Are you a Christian?"

"No."

"Or a Muslim?"

"No. I have no religion."

"When you speak of God, what God do you mean?"

"I do not know, Bwana. 'God' is a word that is used by all people whether they have the Book or not. It is fate or chance. It is the thing that decides which way a coin will fall; whether a child be a boy or a girl, whether it will rain or no."

"But all those objects . . .?" I began.

"People here are simple people," he said. "Rain-making is

work, like being a carpenter or a mason or a fisherman. It is a way of earning a living. Like a carpenter, a rain-maker must have his skill and his tools. Some of those objects have a real use—others are for effect only. That I can tell you. Which ones are of use and which ones are for effect I cannot tell you."

He went on: "Only God can make rain. The skill of a rain-maker lies in knowing before other people when it will rain. Some of these objects help me know this, but mostly I watch the birds and the animals and the plants. From them I learn more than from these"—he touched the bag—"but," he added with a fragile smile, "they make a good impression."

The old man was tired, and although there were many questions I still wanted to ask I let him go. He walked slowly away from the circle of firelight. A hyena yowled in the distance and the cicadas drummed and chattered in the trees.

Early in the morning, five days later, the wind changed. During the day the clouds built up over the hills and during the night the first heavy drops of rain began to fall. What wakened me was not so much the sound of rain on the roof. It was the potent, fecund smell of the earth receiving and absorbing the rain. From the village and the huts in the valley came the sound of drums and of laughter and the collective whinnying of the women. Soon the heavy individual drops became merged in a steady downpour. The rain went on all night.

Shortly after midnight there were noises outside the house. I lit a lamp and went to the door. Outside, standing alone in the slanting rain, was a girl. Beyond her on the fringes of the lamp's range I could see the shadows and hear the murmurings of her supporters. Round her neck the girl wore a single strand of coloured beads. On each wrist and ankle were double rows of cowry shells and round her waist was a triple row of the same coloured beads. In her arms was a chicken, its legs tied with a piece of string. It looked very pale and bedraggled against the smooth glistening darkness of the girl's body. When I opened the door the girl bowed her head and held out the chicken to me. She clapped her hands softly and waited. Then, laughing in the rain, she turned and ran back to her companions.

The next morning I sent a messenger up to Alani with a small package. In it were the fifty-shilling-notes which I had taken up with me on my own visit but which I had not in the end given to him. I explained they were for him to buy a new blanket. I also included a very worn set of poker dice, the purpose of which I did not attempt to explain.

There is a tailpiece to this story. The goats and the beer I had taken to Alani had been provided by the women. The notes which I had sent up to him came from my own pocket. At the end of the month, when we made up the District Office accounts, I recorded a debit of fifty shillings against my contingencies vote "for services rendered by Alani the rain-maker."

Six months later came a query from the Audit Department. It said: "Please state exact nature of services rendered."

One of the clerks had had a small difference of opinion with one of his wives and he was off duty for several days. So I told the messenger, who had started to learn both English and typing as a side-line, what reply to send. Back it came, laconic and beautifully typed, for me to sign. It simply said: "He made water."

I signed it and sent it off. And to my surprise we never heard another word.

CHAPTER TWENTY-SIX

Murder on the River

IN this District, as well as the hills where it was green and cold at night, there was a plain with a large river, and here it was hot and steamy by day, and worse by night.

I spent more time travelling in the hills where, fortunately, most of the people lived, than on the plain. But I went there sometimes, and whenever I went there something unexpected happened.

The tent showed up against the dark mass of the fig trees, and as we walked down through the long brittle grass we got glimpses of the river, like flashes of polished metal, between the green.

The sun was near setting and a long, long distance away it touched the snow on Kilimanjaro with a brief brush of colour.

As the pinks and mauves faded they left a cold, neutral grey behind them. But here in the plain by the river the heat still held and the sweat trickled down the broad brown backs of the men in front of me.

The camp looked just as we had left it early that morning. The cook was still crouched over his fire. The same twos and threes of women were selling eggs and milk, haggling with quick laughter and slow graceful movements of their arms. But, as we got nearer, I saw that one thing was different.

A dozen yards from the tent a tall figure stood on one leg. The second leg was held bent and resting on the other knee. The man was leaning easily on a long iron spear. He looked as if he had been there for hours and could, if need be, stay there for many more.

I had been walking most of the day and I wasn't in the mood for strangers. I had a bath and after that I had some tea. It was some time before I asked who the man was.

The men with me were hill people and they regarded the people who lived across the river with suspicion and some awe. They were as different in looks and dress and ways as an Eskimo from a Londoner.

"He won't talk to us," they said. "He wants to see you, Bwana."

"About what?" I asked. I was still feeling a bit unsociable.

"I don't know. He just says he must speak to you."

When he came up to me he stuck his spear in the ground. He cleared his throat and spat carefully to within a few inches of where his spear still quivered slowly in the earth. Now he was ready to begin.

"The old men sent me," he explained.

I said nothing and he went on.

"They thought it better so."

"What happened?" I asked. This sort of talk could, I knew go on for hours.

"I will explain." He was being very patient.

"Could the story wait until the morning?"

He considered this for some time. In the end he nodded.

"Yes," he said. He still sounded rather doubtful. Then he said it again with more certainty. "Yes, it could wait. It is, after all, over a year since we killed him."

He saluted me gravely and took his spear out of the ground. He walked off towards a clump of trees, and only then did I see that standing beneath them were four or five others of his kind.

In the morning they were waiting for me in the same place. There were five of them altogether.

Apart from the man I had spoken to the night before there was another young man of about the same age and build, two wizened old men and a girl.

This time it was the old men who did the talking. They had bony emaciated faces of distinction and much dignity. Like the young men they wore cotton blankets tied over one shoulder and falling loosely to the knees. It was not exactly a modest garment, but they looked very fine in them.

The girl didn't speak at all. She wore a complicated garment of hides embroidered with beads. Her arms and legs were long and slim and her skin was the colour of pale sherry.

One of the elders started off just where the young man had finished the night before.

"Yes," he said, "we killed him about a year ago."

"And now," he added, "we feel that we ought to settle the matter."

Nearly two years before the girl had been married to a man

138

called Ariopi. He wasn't a young man by any means and a few months afterwards he died.

"How did he die?" I asked.

I looked at the girl while the old man thought about the matter. Her expression gave nothing away. Her eyes were veiled behind long curling eyelashes. Her toes scuffled the dust. Just before I looked away she raised her eyelashes and for a brief fraction of a moment our eyes met.

I wondered just how she had disposed of him.

"He just died," the old man explained at last. "He wasn't very strong."

When the husband died a problem arose. According to the custom of these people a bereaved wife, whatever her age, became the responsibility of the husband's brothers, or if there were no brothers, of his cousins or his uncles. Sometimes this was a pleasure and sometimes it was just a nuisance. But it was a duty and it was accepted.

There was a lot to be said for this custom. In the harsh nomadic conditions under which they lived there was no room for a widow. Every woman must be linked with someone who would protect and feed her and house her. In return she would cook and draw water and carry. Alone, if she were young, she could only go to the bad. There was nothing else for her to do. If she were old she would starve. The missionaries didn't like it, of course, but these people at least didn't take missionaries very seriously . . .

The trouble in this case was that there were two brothers and both of them were only too willing to take on this particular burden. Custom on this point varied from clan to clan, and indeed from time to time. Some said it was the eldest brother's right if she was nice and his duty if she was nasty. Others said the widow herself could choose.

There was a lot of argument.

"The elder brother wanted the girl," the old man explained, "but women," he pointed a bony finger at the girl, "women are perverse like a donkey who wants to go the other way. She wanted to go to the younger brother."

He pointed to the other young man. He was over six feet tall and his skin shone like polished copper.

In the end when the elder brother tried to take her by force she ran away.

She ran away to her own brothers. "That," he pointed at the man who had been waiting for me the night before, "that is one of them.

"The elder brother followed her. He was angry. When he arrived at the place where the girl was he said several things. Some of them were not," he hesitated for the right word, "were not polite.

"One of her own brothers picked up his spear and threw it. It went right through him from here . . . to here." His hands sketched the journey of the spear with a gesture. His face remained impassive and detached. "By the morning he was dead."

I got up and walked through the screen of trees to the bank of the river. They followed me. On the far side there was a crocodile lying on a sloping sandbank. I shouted, and when they brought the rifle I shot him carefully through the heart. It was an easy shot, but all the same it was impressive.

If one wants to show off, crocodile are just the thing. If you hit them almost anywhere they will leap into the air in a very dramatic way and this always creates a very good impression, and no one will bother much whether you meant to hit him there or not. If, on the other hand, you shoot them in the brain or the heart it is impressive in another way. In this case the crocodile didn't move at all. But after a moment or two the jaws opened slowly like a creaking door: as slowly they shut and then the corpse turned over and slid into the river.

I was playing to the gallery and the gallery responded with some nice appreciative grunts. I saw now roughly where this story was leading to. I thought I needed some encouragement. A very nasty baby was, I suspected, soon going to be landed in my lap.

I turned to the young man of the night before.

"Was it you that killed him?" I asked.

I heard the muttering between the two men and I saw the scornful smile on the girl's mouth. I realized I had said the wrong thing.

"No," he said. He was very polite but I could see he was rather shocked.

"No," he repeated, "of course not."

After a long pause he added the appendix.

"It was not as simple as that," he said. "It was my brother who killed him."

I was getting out of my depth.

"And where is your brother?"

"He is dead."

"Did they kill him?" I asked. I pointed at the other youth and at his supporting elder. It was clear that they were related in some way or another.

The other old man took up the tale. He belonged to the family of the girl and her brother.

"No," he said, "that is the trouble. If they had killed him everything would be all right. There would be no need for us to come to you for help. It would have been a fair exchange. A life for a life.

"The difficulty is," he went on, "that after the killing

he ran away. Three days later we found his body in some bushes."

There was a pause—and then I asked another silly question.

"How do you know he wasn't followed and killed by them?" I pointed again at the other elder.

"Because, Bwana," he spoke slowly, as to a backward child, "because if they had they would have told us. They would have told everybody. It was, after all, their duty to kill him to make things even. From the marks it was probably a lion that killed him.

"The trouble now," it was a word they often used, "the trouble now is that things are not even. A man has been killed in one family. They have a score to pay. If it is not settled now it will go on and on, from generation to generation . . ."

The elder took the young man by the elbow and came a pace nearer to me. The others fell back and stood apart, motionless and expectant.

"Take him," the old man said, "take him. Let the Government have him and punish him for the killing. When he is hanged the score will be settled and there will be peace between our families."

The others murmured their assent.

"What relation is this young man to you?" I asked the old man.

He did not look at me but his voice didn't falter.

"He is my son."

The next day was a Sunday. I had fixed the time of our meeting again at nine o'clock. I showed them where the sun would be over the trees.

I took one of the old men aside. Then, without turning, he spoke over his shoulder. It was quietly said and very brief but it was quickly obeyed. The two young men and the girl walked away and waited under the trees.

The old men and I talked together for a long time. I learnt a lot of the system of checks and balances which nomadic peoples had evolved over the years to meet the needs and compulsions of their own particular way of life. Much of it might have come straight from the Old Testament. An eye for an eye, a tooth for a tooth was the basis of it, but in their search for unity and peace, and above all stability, they had developed many subtle variations of this theme.

The question now was this. One death had been deliberately caused. The other had been accidental. Therefore they did not balance. The scales must be made even. Either by lightening the load of the one that had been deliberate or by increasing the weight of what had been done by accident.

The first we tried to do by considering the element of provocation. But it was no use, and in the end we had to give it up. Whatever impolite things had been said about the girl, and they had been very impolite, she had erred in running to her brothers, and they had had no right to obstruct the man who came after her, let alone to kill.

Later we talked about the accident.

"Do you know," I asked, "exactly how he died and when?"

There was a long silence. Then one of the elders shook his head. The other grunted his assent with this lengthily considered view.

"All we know for certain is that he was not killed by one of us."

I took a deep breath. I am not by nature a convincing liar. "Then I will tell you how he died and where and when."

The old men showed no surprise or disbelief on their harsh

lined faces. But neither did they give any sign that they believed me.

"The Government," I went on, "has eyes everywhere, and ears and arms. It sees everything, and little happens that it does not come to know."

I knew I was getting pompous. I knew too that these very untrue words had been said and believed and disbelieved many times before.

"He died on the 6th of February at three o'clock in the afternoon." The dates and the times meant nothing to them, but like a doctor who uses long words to describe a headache or a chill they were calculated to impress.

"He died under a baobab tree three hours' walk to the south of the hill you call Ngit."

The old men now began to watch me carefully.

"And he was killed by a bullet like the crocodile yesterday. In the night a lion dragged the body to the bushes where you found him."

"Did the Government shoot him?" one of the old men asked.

I didn't reply. I thought that perhaps I had told enough lies for one day.

I got up. I said we would meet again in the cool of the evening.

As soon as I saw them that evening I knew it was all right.

"The case is finished," they said. We shook hands all round and I watched as they walked away down the river-bank, to the shallow water where they would cross. The young men went ahead side by side with the girl behind them. More slowly the two older men followed. They also walked together.

Afterwards there were two questions I wanted to ask. I

called the police corporal. He was as tall as the young man, more strongly built and very dark of skin.

"Did the old men believe me?" I asked.

"No, Bwana, they did not believe you."

"Then, why . . ." I began.

"They knew you had lied to help them. But they think that when they tell your story to the other elders and the young men it will be believed that the brother was shot by the Government for the murder."

"But if they didn't believe it why should the others?"

The corporal hesitated and coughed.

"They will change it a little to make it better . . ."

I had one other question.

"And how," I asked, "did you find out about the tree and the hill?"

"From the girl," he answered. "In the evenings when the others were asleep we would go looking for wild honey. It was plentiful and it was also very sweet . . ."

CHAPTER TWENTY-SEVEN

Locusts and Wild Honey

FROM the hill you could see how the cultivated land spread out like a fan from the village. The fan was green from the ripening maize and the beans and the cotton, but beyond the limits of the irrigation the land was brown and dusty and dry.

The locusts had come in across the bare, greenless plain, and they were hungry. By the time I got there they were already attacking the maize in the outer fields.

Nowadays they deal with locusts by spraying poison at them from aircraft. But at that time we weren't very well equipped. I arrived with a lorry-load of zinc sheets and a handbook.

"No poison?" they said when I arrived.

"No," I said. I felt rather bad about it. I should, I know, have brought some contribution from Western civilization to help them.

"Thanks be to God!" they said.

I felt much better after that. The trouble with the poison issued by the Agricultural Department was that it was either so strong that the goats ate it and died, or so weak that the chickens pecked open the sacks and flourished. These people were keen keepers of goats.

The Chief of this area was a particular friend of mine. He was a very new and a very young Chief but he was always anxious to do the right thing. He was a slight, gentle-voiced man of about twenty. He had been at a Government school and I used to lend him books to improve his English. Peter Cheyney was his favourite author but he was conscientiously wading through Bagehot on the British Constitution as well.

Although he was new and young and slight, he was far from ineffective. When the next morning I went to the fields to see how the campaign was going, he had almost every able-bodied man, woman and child on the job. Locusts were a serious matter.

The locust goes through several stages between the time that it first emerges from the pupa and becomes mobile on foot, and the time when it develops its flying wings and becomes mobile by air. The problem at the moment was to destroy as many of them as they could while they were still on the ground. Once they started flying there was little the villagers could do but cross their fingers and hope for the best.

They had two methods of dealing with them. Method A was to beat the locusts to death with sticks and branches. Method B was to call in the witch-doctor.

Method B usually involved little or no physical effort and was therefore more popular. Method A, however, often produced better results. Sometimes therefore they tried both methods at the same time. The Chief himself preferred Method A, and it was partly for that reason that I found so many people beating the locusts in the fields. But there was also another reason.

By-passing the Chief, the women, who of course did most of the work, had called in a witch-doctor on the quiet. He was a tiny, wizened old man, who lived by himself in a hut of reeds by the river. He was known as Cha-Cha. His real name however was Sebastian. He had once worked at a Mission as a cobbler and had got himself baptized. That, however, was a long time ago and he now preferred to be called by his other name.

Cha-Cha was a clever man. What made him even more dangerous was a cynical sense of humour. The women had to pay him for his services in advance, partly in kind.

It was one of the women who told me what had happened.

"Cha-Cha stumped and stalked about the fields like a bantam cock. When he was working he always wore a faded red scarf round his head, and the tail of a black and white monkey tied to a string round his waist.

"He muttered to himself all the time. We women kept well to the rear. He was a bad-tempered man and if we got too near he would beat us with the wand of plaited reeds which he carried in his hand.

"He cut some twigs from a special kind of bush and smeared some *dawa* on them." *Dawa* was a very comprehensive word which covered everything from Epsom salts to incense.

"He put the twigs in the ground at the corners of the fields of maize.

"Then quite suddenly he walked away. He went towards the river where he lived. We thought he had finished and we stayed where we were.

"But he hadn't finished. He turned and signalled us to follow him. When he reached the large fig tree which grows by the river he sat down. We squatted on our heels in a circle round him.

" 'Women,' he said.

" 'Eh——' we answered once more. 'We are listening.'

" 'I have made a powerful spell. The locusts will march to your fields but when they reach the first stalks of maize they will turn.'

" 'Oh——' we all said. We weren't quite convinced but we were pleased.

" 'They will turn, I say, and they will go and eat the maize in the fields of your neighbours.'

" 'Ah——' we said.

"We were very pleased. This was even better than we had hoped for. We didn't like our neighbours. Especially the women . . . Very stuck up they were.

" 'But . . .' The word had a sinister ring. We didn't like the sound of it at all.

"Cha-Cha waited until there was no sound from the crowd. If one of us moved or even scratched he glared at us.

" 'But,' he went on, 'the spell will only work if you do what I tell you.'

"A hush had fallen over the crowd of women. They didn't know what was coming but they sensed already that it wasn't very pleasant.

" 'For one week from today,' Cha-Cha said, 'you must not eat wild honey . . .'

"There was a sigh of relief from the crowd. That wasn't so difficult after all.

" 'Nor must you comb or plait your hair . . .'

"They didn't like this so much, but they realized that sacrifices had to be made.

149

" 'Nor,' he concluded with awful finality—

" 'Nor must you make love.'

" 'Eh . . .' said the women in a horrified whisper.

" 'For seven days?' they asked. They couldn't really believe it.

" 'For seven days. If one of you fails in this the locusts will come into your fields and they will eat your maize and your beans to the very roots.'

" 'But . . .' wailed the women.

"Cha-Cha got up.

" 'I have spoken,' he said. And without another word he walked away."

My informant spread her hands and sighed. Her story was finished.

"Yesterday," I said, "when I arrived I saw that the locusts were in your fields . . ."

"Yes," she said. "It is true, Bwana."

"So now," she concluded, "we are killing the locusts with branches and sticks as the Chief says we must. We are very tired."

I saw that I must do something to help with Method A. I unloaded the zinc sheets from the lorry. I had them carried to the fields. We set them out in a semi-circle, joining them together and fixing them in the ground with pointed metal clasps. At the apex of the semi-circle the men dug some pits. They were about twenty feet wide and about three feet deep.

The men appointed as the killers sat on the edge of the pit, waiting. They held flat rams made of wood.

Everyone else gathered in a wide arc. The young men and the most active women were in front and when they were ready they started to move forward, driving the locusts forward with branches and a great deal of noise. The children, and the old people, and the women with babies on their backs we used as moppers-up. They went behind the solid, moving front line of people and branches and noise, and they killed the clumps and patches of locusts which escaped. They stamped on them with their feet or beat them with branches. On the backs of the women the babies, wide-eyed with excitement, gurgled and crowed their encouragement.

Bit by bit we drove the main masses of the locusts towards the semi-circle of metal sheets. By the time we had them trapped there were several layers of them, one on top of the other, crawling and hopping away from the advancing line and towards the pits. The men were standing up now, the wooden rams already poised in their hands. When the pits were half-full of locusts they started to kill them.

We worked until the sun had set. When it was over the people walked back to the village, the children running in front, laughing and shouting; the others tired but not too tired to sing of their exploits and of the locusts they had so bravely and so fiercely trapped and killed.

Early next morning I went out again. I wanted some statistics.

In one of the pits I measured out a square six inches by six inches, and then we started to count the corpses. It took a long time. We must have looked very silly and I was glad no one was watching. When we had a rough figure I sat down under a tree with a pencil and some paper. The working out took me almost as long as the counting. Cubic capacity was never one of my strong subjects. In the end I calculated that we had killed over three million locusts.

That sounded very fine. But later I went out into the bush beyond the fields where new invasions of our enemy were massing. I couldn't count them when they were alive, but it was easy to see that we had done no more than nibble at the edge of the problem. There were millions upon millions more of them.

But this new version of Method A had made a good impression, and men and women from the neighbouring villages and from the hills began to come in and help us. Each day we staked our semi-circle of zinc sheets in a different place and at the end of each session the piled, squashed millions of locusts filled the pits. They smelt a bit, of course, and the air was full of excited, questing birds.

A few days later the Chief came to me with a long expression on his round, serious face. We talked for a bit, and then we went out into the bush beyond the cultivated fields. Behind us came a straggle of experts.

"Look," the Chief said.

Every small tree and every thorny thicket was festooned with locusts. For the most part they hung motionless but now and then one would twist and turn with urgent, compelling purpose. As they moved they glistened in the sun. On the ground the masses of insects coming in from the plain no longer moved purposefully towards the crops. They crowded and crawled together in lethargic, seething groups.

"In two days," one of the experts said, "they will be ready to fly."

He took me by the arm and pointed at one of the locusts on a bush. One more twist and it was free. Its old skin hung from the new, shining head, and folded limply along its sides over the wings.

"When they are dry and strong he will fly. He and a million others."

All around us the locusts were casting their old skins. Yesterday they were hoppers, restricted to the ground. Tomorrow they would try their wings, and the next day they would be free to fly over the plains and the hills, and if need be the sea.

"Today and tomorrow," the experts said, "we can still kill them on the ground. And then . . ." They spread their hands flat, the fingers wide.

"And then . . . it will be as God wills."

We sent messages to the villages in the hills for more men. Some, but not many, had already come. But without enthusiasm. It was too cold in the hills at night for the hoppers and at this stage, therefore, their crops were not threatened. But once the locusts were flying, then they, too, they knew, would be in danger.

The response this time was good. The men came down from the hills early the next morning. They wore blankets over their shoulders and they had sticks and spears in their hands. Many carried knives and machetes. Some had children with them; and patches of colour and laughter that were girls, brought, it seemed, to encourage and to chide rather than to work. One man brought an old muzzle-loading gun. It looked as if the locusts were in for a difficult time on their last day.

Only from one area in the hills did no one come. It was thickly wooded there and the crops grew in clearings in the forest. "The locusts never visit us," they said. "And if we leave the crops the baboon and the pig and the birds will eat them."

It was not until the sun was up over the hills on the following day that the locusts began to fly. They whirred first of all in low, short flights, and came to ground again. Then they went up again, higher this time, and circled.

We watched from the slope of the hill. The experts muttered to themselves and scuffled their bare toes in the dust.

The third time they rose they moved in towards the hills

and caught the upward currents of air that followed the line of the slopes. They rose from an area of about twenty miles in length and none of us knew how far it stretched into the depth of the plain. As they moved they crossed the line of the sun and cast a pale, freckled shadow over the watching faces.

It was some time before the people began to realize that the locusts had passed over the green of their fields and were heading for the hills. The swarms rose higher and higher, and were lost to sight. Whispers grew to cries and cries to shouts.

"They have gone. They have gone," the men said. "They have run away. They are frightened." The women added a touch of scorn to their relief.

We watched the swarms until the sky was empty and the sun threw no more freckled shadows on our faces. Some of the locusts we noted had headed to where the hills were wooded, and the men had stayed to chase away baboon and pig.

The woman who had told me about Method B was standing under a tree in a group of other women. As I passed them on my way I made the usual greeting.

The woman replied and laughed, and spat precisely in the dusty earth.

"I wonder," she said, "if Cha-Cha was also called by the women where the hills are wooded."

And as it happens I was wondering the same thing.

CHAPTER TWENTY-EIGHT

The New Chief

THE last time I saw the old Chief he had looked like a
very ancient and a very wrinkled tortoise. Even to the shell.
He was cold as he felt death creeping up towards him and he
wore a blanket. It had a pattern of squares but age and dust and
dirt had turned the patterned cloth into a thick grey carapace.
The lids hung heavily over dull, yellowed eyes and when he
opened his mouth to whisper a greeting and a farewell it was
parched and dry and cracked.

I could barely hear the words.

"Go in peace," he said, "until we meet again."

I knew I would never see him again: and so did he. But it
would have been a breach of propriety to have allowed the fact
to colour our words or our demeanour. He had a Christian
name: but as he travelled towards the grave he turned more

and more to the habits and beliefs and rituals of his own people. With all their faults and fallacies, and he was aware of them, he was in the end more sure of these older things, because, he once told me, their roots went deeper in him.

I wanted too to talk to him of the succession. Who was to follow him was I knew a difficult and complicated matter, and one that could lead to bitterness and strife. But I could not ask him. That too would have been a breach of propriety.

A few weeks later the first emissaries came to see me. There were nine of them, but it was the tall, thin man who did all the talking.

"He has died."

His voice was curiously high-pitched, and his hands moved restlessly to emphasize every phrase.

"He has died, and now we have no Chief.

"He has six sons," he went on.

"Six?" I asked.

"Six." He held up the five fingers of one hand and a thumb to support the figure. The others muttered their agreement. "Yes," they said, "it is indeed the truth."

I did not doubt it. I only marvelled that they should know. The old Chief had been a strong family man. He had in his time had many wives and many more acquaintances, and sometimes the borderline between them had been ill-defined.

"As you know, Bwana," he went on, "the custom is that we the elders of the people should choose which son should be the Chief.

"We have thought deeply about the matter and now we have made our choice."

I wondered how much beer had been consumed during the process and what presents and promises and threats had been offered and accepted and rejected. But I didn't say anything.

"We have chosen well."

"Yes," I said. They wanted me to become curious and impatient and to ask. The sun threw back its heat and its glare from the bare stony hillside and the flies buzzed on the window panes.

In the end he said the name.

"It is Vincenti."

They added a vowel to the word so that it fitted easily into the tongue.

I knew Vincent. He had a tawdry, dissolute face, but he was full of guile. I didn't like him very much. Vincent was not the eldest son. The eldest was a pleasant, ingenuous unclever man. He would not have made a good chief. The most able one was unfortunately in gaol.

The next delegation came two days later. There were three of them. One was a very old man who said nothing but he had a good repertoire of expressive noises of assent and dissent. The other two were well dressed, smooth, sophisticated young men. It was a long time before they came to the point.

"Eleven generations ago," they started, "a man called Kaliwa quarrelled with his father. They lived over there." They pointed to the blue silhouette of hills far away to the north.

"He fled to this country and took a wife of the people who lived here. He was a rain-maker of remarkable ability and in the end they asked him to be their Chief."

The young man who was doing the talking was a good speaker. He was a schoolmaster, and he wore glasses that were designed to impress rather than to improve his sight.

"According to the customs of his tribe Kaliwa carried three

notches cut into the skin of his face along the line of the cheek-bone. These marks were made on the faces of his children, both the boys and the girls, and they in the time when they married and had children cut the same marks on the faces of their offspring. And so it was continued, generation after generation.

"When the Germans came to this country," he went on, "a man with these same marks was Chief. His name too was Kaliwa. But the Germans did not like him. They deposed him and later his body was found in the bottom of a well."

He paused then. The old man made a sorrowful, nostalgic sound. Soon, I thought now, they would come to the point.

"In his place they put another man as Chief. His name was Pakulagi. The Chief who has just died was his grandson." He turned then and took the old man by the arm. He put up a show of modest resistance like a new speaker in the House of Commons, but it didn't last very long.

"This is the rightful Chief. Look, here are the marks."

The third delegation came the next day. It wasn't a large party, but it was very colourful. Even the old woman was swathed in vivid, purple cloth. The girl was a lithe, handsome creature, in stripes of scarlet and green.

Their story was also colourful. It took a long time to tell and when the old lady grew hoarse the girl would take up the tale, and vice versa. It was complicated, and it was studded with fascinating jewels of very indelicate detail.

"I was the dead Chief's first wife," the older one explained in her parched, cracked voice.

"He was a good, strong man then, a veritable goat of a man, but by the time he started looking for a second wife he was finished . . ."

This is a rather condensed version of what she actually said but it covers the gist of it.

"The second wife, and the third, and the others, were just for show. The children they had were not his children. They, too, were just for show."

The girl in the scarlet and green stripes added a comment of her own. It was not the sort of thing one would ordinarily expect a granddaughter to say.

For that was what she was. The first wife had had several children, and they were all, she said, of the chiefly blood. But they had all been girls. Except one. His name was Labigo. He had married when he was about twenty and soon afterwards he had died. The girl was his only child.

"You see therefore," the girl herself now took up the story as it leaped from indiscretion to indiscretion to its clear conclusion, "that I am the only true claimant to the vacant chair. My father was the only male child the dead Chief himself begat. And by custom I, my father's only child, am the proper heir."

There was a silence in the room that even the clerks in the other room could hear. The typewriter ceased its chattering and the buzz of conversation faded to a whisper.

"I see," I said. There didn't seem anything else to say.

In the end it was decided by the powers-that-be to play safe. The choice of the elders was accepted and in due course I went again up into the hills to accord Vincent formal recognition. It was, I felt, what most of the people expected and wanted: but as I drove up the winding road I knew that some of them still held a different view and had not entirely given up hope that things might yet be altered.

I took two policemen with me. One was a corporal of six

foot two, and the other was a sturdy, phlegmatic character, who was good with crowds and could deal with backchat like a barmaid. They both came from other tribes.

I put up my tent on the village green where the schoolboys played football in the evenings and where, when the moon was full, dances of sorts took place which were governed by rules that had never been codified and where no whistles were sounded by the referee.

On another flat piece of ground not very far away were gathered the supporters of Kaliwa and his clan. There were about three hundred of them, I was told, and they were not in a co-operative mood. Of the old woman and her granddaughter there was no sign. But I had a feeling that I hadn't seen the last of them.

The ceremonies involved in installing the new Chief were of two kinds. The first were the complicated, long-established rituals of the tribe. They started early in the morning and I did not attend them. The other was a brief, artificial gathering in the brick meeting-place, where I would formally accept the new man as the Chief recognized by the Government, and where the elders and the heads of the various clans that made up this section of the tribe would endorse the choice.

When we heard them coming down the track that shone in the sun from the polish of the naked feet that for days and years and scores of years had trod the bare, red earth, I walked up to the flat spur just opposite the hill where Kaliwa's people were assembled. The path curved round the base of the hill, and from it they could see and sneer. From it too, if so minded, they could spit and stone. I took the corporal and the other man with me.

But in the end they didn't sneer or spit or throw stones. As the procession wound round the base of the hill, and we watched a little anxiously from the other side, Kaliwa's men pulled their blankets across their faces and with carefully measured incivility they turned their backs.

I waited until they were all settled in the meeting-house and then I walked up the length of the room to the platform at the end where the Chief and the elders were standing beside their chairs and stools.

There were speeches, of course—long, rambling, historical speeches, and short barks and grunts of support from wrinkled elders, who had smelt the beer which was being brewed under the fig tree outside and feared it would be spoilt with waiting or drunk by others who had no public duties to perform.

The Chief himself, I thought, looked ill at ease, and during the speeches the elders muttered much among themselves.

"Did they go well, the rituals and the ancient ceremonies?" I asked.

The heads nodded assent but the eyes in them were guarded.

"Was something forgotten or left out?" I asked again.

"No, Bwana. Nothing."

But the answer was hesitant and I knew that something had gone wrong.

I concentrated on one old man who had a ready, toothless smile and who had clearly already tasted the ceremonial beer. And bit by bit it came out. Everything it seemed had been done and said and sworn as custom decreed. Except one small thing.

"They couldn't find the *ʒikala*." The old man bent towards me to whisper it.

"What is the *ʒikala*?" I said. I had never heard the word before.

"It is the claw of a lion which the Chief always wears. It is held on a cord round the waist."

"What is its purpose?"

"Ai, ai," was all the old man would say at first, but eventually he told me.

"It is to bring fertility. To the Chief and to our people and our land."

It was nearly time for me to say my piece and I had to leave the matter there. When I had spoken, the formal business of the day would end and people would disperse to sing and dance and drink the new Chief in.

But it wasn't quite the end after all.

As I got up to leave a figure detached itself from the crowd. The old woman was still gaily dressed but the colours were different and I didn't recognize her at first. But the voice when she started to speak was very familiar. I had heard it before, at length.

In a few short sentences she demolished the fabric of the day.

"He is a bastard," would be an over-simplification of what she actually said, but that was roughly the sum of it.

"This," her hand reached into the crowd behind her, "this is the rightful heir."

The girl was still swathed in scarlet and green stripes and could not be mistaken.

"Look at her, you people of the hills. Look at the only true offspring of the dead Chief's loins."

The girl pushed past the old women and held the stage. The crowd creased and stiffened in expectant silence, and behind me the new Chief and the elders stood in their tracks and waited . . .

They hadn't long to wait. The green and scarlet cloth lay suddenly on the beaten earth and the taut body rose out of it like a statue in shiny polished wood.

"The *zikala*. The *zikala*." The word was not spoken, but each man said it to himself till it could be sensed in the hot, still air. The white cord showed clearly against the girl's skin and the claw shone maliciously and mockingly at the shocked, gaping crowd.

The angry muttering had already started when the sturdy, phlegmatic constable, who was good with crowds, reached the centre of the room. With a few brief words he, in turn, demolished the fabric of the interruption. They were in very poor taste and quite unprintable. But the roars of laughter they evoked confirmed the new Chief in his office more surely than anything I had done that day.

And when order had been restored he somehow had the lion's claw in his hand.

"The cord can be replaced," the new Chief said. And clutching the symbol in a somewhat sweaty, trembling hand, he strode out of the meeting-place to take up his inheritance.

CHAPTER TWENTY-NINE

The Dead Witch-Doctor

H E CAME quite suddenly out of the trees into the flicker-
ing circle of firelight. I watched him as he walked across
to where the porters were huddled in their blankets round the
other fire. I wondered who he was.

We had camped in a clearing in the forest. It was cold in the
hills at night and they had lit the brushwood fires before the
sun went down. In the distance the mountains had turned a
dark silhouetted blue before they merged into the darkness.

He wanted to see me about something, they said. Something
he wouldn't speak of but it was important. He stood some way
away until my messenger had gone. Then he came forward.

"I heard that you were looking for me." He spoke slowly with a country man's aversion to words and eloquence.

"Yes," I said. I had no idea who he was or why he had come: but he seemed to need encouragement.

"Yes," he went on. "I ran away but now I have come back."

I saw that on each side of his head beside the eyes he had two small grooves cut into the much-lined ochre-coloured skin. He was not a young man but he was tall and lithe and all his movements and gestures were quiet and sure.

"What is your name?" I asked.

"I am called Ingalitawa. I live over there." He pointed into the dark cloud of trees.

I still didn't know who he was.

There was a long silence. Then he cleared his throat and turned his head aside to spit into the fire.

"I ran away and now I have come back."

He repeated what he had said before. I realized that he thought I was being rather stupid.

"Why did you run away?" I asked. I thought I must get to the bottom of this before he gave me up as a bad job and walked away back into the trees.

"Why did I run away?" He sounded incredulous. "Because I killed him."

It was stated simply as a plain, ordinary fact.

"Why did you kill him?" Now that I was asking straight, sensible questions he came closer. It was clear that he wanted to help.

"Why did I kill him?" He repeated my question. "Because he was a bad man. A very bad man."

"What did he do?" I said.

"He was a witch-doctor."

Now I knew who he was. I called and told them to give him

some food and a place to sleep by the fire. He saluted me gravely with hand upraised and walked with unhurried dignity across the clearing.

Some weeks before a man had been found dead in a patch of bush behind the village. He had been stabbed. The knife was still between his ribs when they found him but no one knew whose knife it was.

The dead man's name was Koti. At first no one would talk about him but bit by bit it came out. People had been frightened of him. They were still frightened of him although he was dead.

He had been a man who, like his father before him, dealt in potions and spells. Like many people of his kind in Africa he had mainly used his powers to help people—to bring good luck in hunting and in love. To cure the sick and to scare away bogies and bad dreams. But an ugly wasting disease had turned him into a sour, bitter man, and in his latter years he had done little but evil.

We had no idea who had killed him. So many people hated him that we didn't know where to start.

The next night we camped in a fold of the hills. It overlooked the flat endless plain below. In the distance we could see the meandering line of trees which marked the river.

After I had had supper I called for Ingalitawa. I told him to sit down and he folded himself cross-legged beside the fire. He held his blanket across his chest and I saw that two of the fingers on his left hand were missing.

"I was chopping wood," he explained. "I made a mistake." He held his hand vertically to show how old he had been. "I was only a child," he explained.

It was some time before we got round to the subject of murder. One had, I felt, to observe certain decencies in an important matter of this kind.

"Why did I kill him?" he repeated my question. He paused before he gave his reply.

"I did not like him, Bwana."

I didn't say anything and later he went on.

"I have a wife. She is a woman but she is strong and she works well. She has borne four children. Good healthy children." He held up his right hand to show the number with his fingers.

"The last time she was with child she tripped and fell. When the baby was born it was dead.

"That was the first thing."

A touch of drama had come into his voice, and I felt a small chill creep like a lizard into the air.

"Later," he went on again, "I was out hunting for honey in the forest. Climbing a tree I put my hand on a snake lying concealed in the branches. It bit me. For many days I was very sick. I thought I would die.

"That was the second thing.

"A short time ago," he continued, "one of my children became ill. His stomach swelled up and he vomited. After two days he fell down and died.

"That was the third thing."

I was glad of the warmth and the light of the fire. The trees seemed to have crept a little closer: to have become a little darker.

When he spoke again his voice was lower. I could barely hear him.

"Then I knew that I had been bewitched. I and my family. I went off into the forest alone to think. And then I came to know it was Koti."

"How did you know?" I asked.

He sat silent and brooding before he answered my question.

"I cannot explain. I just knew.

"You see, Bwana," he continued, "many years ago my father's father and Koti's father had a quarrel. It was a quarrel over a piece of land . . ."

The story went on for a long time. It was very detailed and very complicated. It was full of the passion evoked everywhere by disputes over small pieces of unfertile land. It might have happened in the further parts of Cornwall.

It was late when he had finished talking. Some of the porters were already snoring by their fire. As I walked across to my tent I trod on a little piece of wood and started in foolish unreasoning alarm. As I lay in bed I thought of Ingalitawa saying, "That was the first thing" and of the chill that had come into the air.

The last night we spent under a clump of wild fig trees at the foot of the hills.

"But how do you know," I asked him, "that Koti is to blame? His father had a quarrel with your grandfather. That I know. That this quarrel has been handed down from father to son, I understand that too. It happens everywhere. But the stillborn baby, the snake, the death of the child. They are things that might happen to us all."

"You do not understand, Bwana." It was not offensive. He was simply stating a fact.

"For everything that happens there are two causes. When a man dies we usually know the immediate cause. A disease, or a fall or a blow.

"But," he went on, "there is always the other cause. When a man falls and breaks his neck what is it that made him fall?

When he dies of fever what is it that made him and not his neighbour get the fever? When my wife bore a dead child I knew it was the fall that did it. But why did she trip and not her sister?

"When a succession of bad things happens to a man he must look for this other cause. And if he does not find it and destroy it, it will destroy him and all that belongs to him."

There were things one could say to this. But when he had finished I didn't want to say them. I stood up then and he also got to his feet.

"It may be so," I said, "but to kill a man is wrong. It is against the law. It is a sin."

"I know, Bwana," he replied. "I know the law, and I am not afraid to die. But to kill is perhaps not always a sin. When other people do bad things we all click our tongues and say how terrible they are. But when for some reason we do them ourselves somehow——" He spread his hands in a wide uncomprehending gesture—"somehow they seem to be right and natural."

I had to prepare the case myself, and when it was ready with the exhibits and the witnesses, such as there were, we sent him for trial by the High Court in one of the big towns. These things took a long time and I had other matters to think about.

When months later he walked into my office late one afternoon I couldn't for a moment think who it was.

"I am Ingalitawa," he said.

I was surprised to see him and pleased, and I got up to take his hand. But before I did so I thought I had better ask a few questions.

"Have you run away from prison?"

I meant it as a joke but he didn't smile. He shook his head. "No, Bwana."

"But the case," I asked, "is it finished?"

"Yes, Bwana. It is finished."

He coughed and looked for somewhere to spit. He knew that offices weren't equipped for proper conversation.

"They let me off," he spoke the words awkwardly as if he had done something to be ashamed of.

"I told them that I had killed him but"—he spread his hands apologetically—"they wouldn't believe me."

"Did they explain why?" I asked him.

"Yes. They said a lot of words. They said I had no proper motive. That there were no witnesses. I do not understand the ways of your law."

Now I felt free to shake his hand. But his face was sorrowful. He looked a worried man. As he turned to go he said,

"Bwana?"

"Yes. What is it?"

"You believe I killed him, don't you? You believe I was speaking the truth?"

"Yes. I believe you."

He looked relieved. When he walked out of the door he seemed happier.

A few moments later he came in again. I think he had probably gone out to spit in comfort.

The worried look was back on his face.

"There is one more thing."

I waited for him to go on.

"I have done a bad thing. To kill Koti was not bad. But this other thing is very bad, truly bad. And I did not tell you about it."

"Tell me then," I said. I knew he must have gone through

a difficult time before and during and after the trial in the alien town.

"It is about the knife I killed Koti with."

"Yes." I waited. I had a lot of other things to do, but I wanted to see this through to the end.

"I stole it. I stole it from a shop."

After he had gone I went to the window. He hadn't stayed to talk with anyone. He was walking down the dusty road, his blanket folded about him and his eyes were fixed on the trees in the distant blue hills where he lived.

CHAPTER THIRTY

Election Day

CHACAMO was an old-fashioned man. He had eleven wives and, he told me vaguely but with pride, many tens of children. He held up his two fists and extended all the fingers. He did this several times and then let his hands fall away. Once he had made his point in a general way he seemed to lose interest in the detail. He wore a furry cap made from the hide of a gazelle, and he always carried a long smooth staff. He was an old man now and he often used it for support.

"Why?" he had asked. "For what reason?"

I wasn't very sure of the answer myself. But it was something that had to be done. And if it had to be done there had to be some reasons for it.

"Well . . ." I began. "All the men of your people pay taxes. Is it not right that they should have a say in how the money should be spent?"

"No," said Chacamo.

"Your Elders," I went on, "are all old men. When you want advice you ask them. Is it not right that the young men, the teachers, the traders, those who have been to school, is it not right that you should ask their advice also?"

"No," said Chacamo again.

"The women," I concluded, "they do all the work. They bear the children. They brew the beer. Is it not fair that they should have a voice in the affairs of your people?"

"A voice?" said Chacamo. "A voice? Their voice is already a shout. Do you wish it to be any louder?"

I had introduced this to give him a point. We had never really intended that the women should have a vote. To start with at any rate. But the only effect of my subtlety was to convince him finally that I was just a bit stupid.

We arranged to have the elections later in the month. Democracy had arrived. But only just. It had arrived as a matter of fact in the last mail but one from headquarters. And now I was doing the rounds of the Chiefs in the District explaining to them what was to happen.

"You will have a Council," I said, "to help you with the affairs of your people. And the members of the Council will be elected by the people themselves."

None of the Chiefs thought much of the idea.

Where the road crossed the stream there were half a dozen wild fig trees. They were large generous trees and under them many scores of people could get shelter from the sun.

Chacamo sat on a stool under one of the fig trees. Behind

him the Elders squatted on the ground. Some of them chewed tobacco, with distant ruminating expressions on their gaunt lined faces. And periodically they would spit. In the manner of their spitting they expressed exactly and concisely what they felt.

"It is the end of us," the spitting said. "But let us face the end with dignity and with disdain."

Chacamo said nothing. We watched the proceedings carefully. Despite himself he was interested and he was wondering too how he could use this new alien custom to serve his own chiefly ends.

When I called for the first candidate no one moved. I called again: and still no one came forward. I looked towards the fig tree where Chacamo and the Elders were. I saw Chacamo flick his fingers and one of the Elders rose and walked towards me.

He was the first candidate.

One by one, after that, five others came forward. One was a young shopkeeper, a well-fleshed, self-confident man. Many people in the area owed him small sums of money. I thought he would probably get in.

Two were schoolmasters. Eloquent, pleasant-mannered men, who had been to Government or Mission schools. When one of them stepped forward a group of girls, spectators in yellow and green and scarlet cloth, clapped softly. The other two were middle-aged men. One I already knew as a strident trouble-making lawyer of the bush, but he never beat his wife and no one respected him. The other man owned large numbers of cattle and had a cleft palate. He looked a likely candidate, I thought.

I called out once more in case there were others too shy or too uncertain to come forward.

Slowly a figure came out of the crowd. It was an old,

old woman with arms and legs like shiny matchsticks. Irregular patches of wiry white hair showed against the skull like pieces of furze that had escaped a fire. She walked slowly across the open space in a hushed expectant silence. When she reached the place where I was standing she stood still for a moment to recover her breath. Then she scratched her ribs and finally she spat, turning her head slightly in a ladylike way.

She wore a kind of skirt. The material had once had a pattern but that was long ago. The top had been doubled over to make it stay up. She started to undo this, and for a moment I thought she wanted to show me some old and honourable scar. But in the end she found what she was looking for. It was a little bag of cloth and in it were three shillings, badly charred.

"They got burnt," she explained.

"Bad luck," I said.

"Yes, Bwana." She clearly had no intention of letting me get away with a mere condolence.

"I want new ones." She held out the burnt silver shillings in her hand.

I took them and gave her three moderately new pieces from my pocket. She examined them carefully, turning them over in her hand before she put them in the small bag. When she had retied her skirt and had a final spit she raised her hand in a sort of half-salute and walked slowly back to her place in the crowd.

No one else came forward so we had six candidates altogether. From this area we wanted two members for the Council. I made a speech explaining the procedure, and then we started.

Each candidate went out and stood by one of the six stones we had put on the ground. At a signal, slowly at first and then more confidently, the voters came forward and stood in single file behind the candidate of their choice. Some of the lines were long and some were very short.

At the head of the shortest line was one of the schoolmasters. The one the girls had clapped. We told him that he was out. He laughed, and we told him and his supporters to go and stand behind whichever of the other candidates they fancied. They mostly joined the line of the other schoolmaster.

This might not be P.R. as recommended in the textbooks but it seemed to meet our needs fairly well. It was after all their first election and very few of them could read and write.

We did the same to the next shortest line and so on until we were down to three. At this stage it wasn't easy to see at a glance which was the shortest so we counted the people in each line, and in the end we got our two members.

One as I had expected was the fat shopkeeper. But the other to my surprise was the wrinkled Elder who had been the first to come forward.

"It is not a bad system," Chacamo conceded when the crowd had dispersed.

The old fox, I thought. I wonder how he did it.

But as it turned out, the wrinkled Elder was a very good Councillor; fair, and astringent and sometimes very witty, and the fat, prosperous-looking shopkeeper, perpetually pursuing his petty debts in public transport, was one of the worst.

CHAPTER THIRTY-ONE

The Road

"I THINK it ought to go this way."

It was said politely but very firmly, and as usual he was right.

We were looking at two ridges in the hills. One was slightly higher than the other and more bumpy. I had thought the lower one would be better. It was more thickly wooded but the slope looked easier. It was, but just out of sight it perversely went downhill again.

Old Man Abi, as he was called, and I were planning the route for a road up into the hills. We had none of the impressive-looking instruments that borough surveyors and proper road-makers employ. This road was being built on the cheap, and in any case neither of us knew how to use them.

It had started several months before. I had been walking in these hills followed by a thin file of thickset porters, and every two or three days I would stop in one of the villages and listen to what the people there had to say.

"Ee——" they said at one place, "life is very hard."

A tall gaunt-faced man stood up at the back of the crowd. He scratched himself carefully on the ribs, and in one or two other places. With a sweep of his hands he called for silence. It was clearly a practised gesture, but it was, as it happens, quite unnecessary, as the crowd was already quiet. Expectantly quiet. This, one sensed, was the village orator.

"Look, Bwana," he started, "look at the fields and gardens where our crops are ripening. You can see the berries in the coffee trees are thick and glossy. The heads of the corn are already full and heavy." His tone implied that any fool could see it. "But does that make us glad?" He asked the question and it was clear that he also intended to answer it.

"No." The word came out flat like cold wet fish on a slab.

The chorus of assent with his dissent spread over the crowd. I wondered if they had been rehearsing.

"Look at our women and girls," he went on. "Look at their sad faces and their bent backs."

The women and the girls were together in another part of the crowd. They bent their heads to hide their bright watchful eyes and the flashes of white teeth. They looked very unsad to me, but they quickly set up a sorrowful moan to endorse their orator.

"In other places when the rains are good and the crops are full the women and the girls rejoice—they sing and dance and clap their hands. But does that happen in these unhappy hills?

"No, Bwana. It does not."

He really was very good, I thought. But I wondered where all this was leading to.

"Well," I said, "why is this so?"

I knew I was expected to ask the question. Otherwise this sort of thing could go on for hours.

"Why, Bwana?" The orator had got his cue. "Why? I will ask the people here. Thus you will hear from them why we are sad and unhappy."

He turned to the crowd.

"Why are you sad, oh people of the hills?" he asked them. "What is it that you want? Tell the Bwana that he may know."

The schoolboys in the front started it. It spread through the men and it was echoed in the shrill whinnies of the womenfolk.

"A road—a road. We want a road."

I could see their point. The valleys in the hills were fertile and they grew coffee and wheat and beans. They grew more than they wanted themselves and they sold the rest in the markets along the road in the plain below. But every bag of corn and every basket of coffee and beans had to be carried there. The journey took six hours and most of the carrying was done by the women. It was the custom. The theory was that the men, handsomely attired, protected the women from hostile tribes and wild beasts. In fact, the hostile tribes and most of the wild beasts had disappeared long ago, but somehow or other the custom had continued. The Elders, who were men, had said so.

Another snag was the things they wanted from the outside world. Lamps and coloured cloth and sugar. They all had to be carried up the hill. Not only was it hard work but it made them very expensive.

"A road—a road. We want a road——"

It may have been rehearsed. But there was certainly a lot to be said for it.

"Not a hope, old boy—not a hope."

I had been trying to get some money for the road. But I hadn't the eloquence of the orator in the hills nor his chorus to help me. I left the office of my higher-ups empty-handed, or almost empty-handed. I came back, however, with a lorry-load of spades and picks, and some sticks of gelignite in a box marked "Keep away from the Boilers."

In the end the men agreed to work for sixpence a day. They would come in shifts for three days at a time and then return to admire their crops and protect their womenfolk.

I had a small allocation of money for filling in potholes on other roads. I used some of this to pay the men their sixpences, and when this ran out I used various other allocations. One I remember was Repairs to Typewriters and another was for Latrines and Washhouses. As it happens we had one or two quite talented masons in our jail at the time.

When Old Man Abi and I had fixed the line of the road we started work. I had originally planned to have some people at the bottom and some at the top at the same time but Abi shook his head.

"No," he said, "that would not be wise."

"But why on earth not?" I asked irritably. It was very hot and I had walked for miles.

He looked at me with his sad yellowed eyes.

"The two parties might never meet. Only God can tell," he added.

So we started at the bottom, while everyone was full of

enthusiasm. Later when perhaps it had waned it would be cooler up there and not so far to walk.

The place where I lived and where I had my office was forty or fifty miles away in the flat country and I had occasionally other things to do. My little parish at that time was about the size of Wales. So, after the first few days, I could only go there once or twice a week.

It was exciting to walk up from the bottom and to see the new road cut into the hillside and to hear the voices of the workmen ahead in the trees and to guess how far they had got. Sometimes, of course, they hadn't got anywhere at all. The men hadn't turned up or there had been an argument or the womenfolk had demanded extra protection, but bit by bit the road crept up into the hills.

One day I arrived to find everyone on strike. This was bad enough—what made it worse was that it was entirely my fault. I had found some strangers hanging about the place where my headquarters were. They were on their way back to their own country and had run out of money. I offered them work on the road and they accepted.

They were strange-looking people. They filed their teeth to sharp points and wore their hair in a stuck-up fuzzy style that made them look as if they were in a permanent state of extreme fright.

There was a lot of shouting and gesticulation and it was some time before I could find out what the trouble was.

"They are savages. They are terrible people."

Everyone talked at once at first, but gradually a spokesman emerged from the people of the hills. He was a rugged character with a broken nose and a withered arm who acted as a sort of timekeeper.

"These people"—he pointed in a superior fashion at the

filed teeth who were leaning on their shovels with rather ostentatious unconcern—"we cannot work with them."

"Don't they work well?" I asked.

It wasn't that. There were no complaints on that score.

"Do they quarrel?" I went on.

No, they said. They kept to themselves and made no trouble.

I wondered what it was. There were some villages near by. In an aside I asked if they were philandering with the girls in the evenings.

"No, no, Bwana." My question had offended them. "Our girls wouldn't have anything to do with savages like these—look at their teeth."

"Well, what is it then?" They liked me to go on guessing at the answer, but I was impatient with the delay. No work seemed to have been done for days.

"We will tell you then." The spokesman came closer to me and whispered the reason. Knowing what he had said all the others muttered a chorus of disapproval and wagged their heads.

"I see," I said.

I held my meeting with the men with the filed teeth a little farther down the road. One by one the others took up their spades and picks and started work—but they worked in twos and threes and chattered anxiously together. They were wondering suspiciously what was going on at my small meeting.

It was slow-going. We were strangers, these people and I, and we barely had a language in common.

"Is the food we give you not enough?" I asked. In addition to the wages of sixpence a day we provided rations.

They nodded. They understood this question.

"Is the food dull, unappetizing, tasteless?" I tried several words. None of them seemed to ring a bell. They just stared in a friendly, helpful manner.

I tried another tack.

"What do you eat in your own country?" I asked.

"Everything," one man replied.

"Everything?" I questioned this as politely as I could. "But . . ."

"Everything." They all replied together this time. One man I saw was quietly dismembering a large dung-beetle.

"Even . . .?" I started.

"Everything," they said again. They were beginning to enjoy themselves.

So I made a rule. In future the filed-teeth contingent had to camp separately and eat separately. I realized that I couldn't stop them eating lizards and beetles and snakes and frogs. It was what they were used to.

"It upsets the others," I explained.

"Upsets?" they said. They couldn't understand it.

"Yes," I said firmly.

"But snakes are good to eat," they said.

"Look," one man added. He pulled one out of his pocket. It was only a small one but it still had a few wriggles in it.

It was time, I thought, that I brought the meeting to an end.

"One thing you must not do," I said. "You must not eat the chameleon. Not even by yourselves."

"Never?" they chorused. They were like small boys deprived of ice-cream for the holidays.

"Never," I said.

"To these people," I went on, pointing at the hill people down the road, "the chameleon has a special meaning. To kill one is a sin. To eat one is . . ."

I couldn't think of a word bad enough.

"Ah," they said. It was a long-drawn-out mournful sound. It almost brought a lump to my throat.

Watercourses were our chief problem. There were a few streams along the route of the road and they had to be bridged. We used timber cut from the hillside, and for the larger ones I managed to scrounge some old girders and spare rails. At least, I hoped they were spare. We found them by the side of the railway line. It was very hot in the plains in the daytime. So we moved them at night when, among other things, it was cooler.

The real trouble were the gullies that only filled up in the rains. We found that the best and cheapest way was to fill them in. The top and the sides had to be faced with stone to prevent them being scoured and washed away, as the water, of course, when it came had to go over the surface.

Some of them took days to fill in. It was very irritating if it rained before they were faced with stone. This only happened once or twice and then we had to start all over again. It was also very irritating when a herd of elephant came down at night and tested our stone walls for strength before they were ready.

But in the end the road was finished. I drove my car up to the top. It boiled but it got there. On the return journey I took half a dozen of the workmen just for the ride. I couldn't take all of them but I did several trips that day to try and narrow the invidious gap between those who had ridden and those who hadn't.

Later that evening we decided to open the road to traffic on a Thursday. There were a few things like small tree stumps that my car had discovered for itself on its several journeys that had to be tidied up before we could say we were really ready. It was obviously important that the first proper journey by a fully laden lorry should be a success.

As I was leaving a man stepped forward.

"You have forgotten something, Bwana," he said.

From the affirmative voices which accompanied this statement it was clear that everyone else thought so too.

I wondered what it was.

I had a moment of panic. I knew there was no more money left.

He coughed slightly and scratched his stomach.

"We did not tell you but this country is haunted."

"Haunted?" I said.

"Yes. Not very much." He spread his fingers to show the extent of it. "Not very much but enough . . ."

"Enough for what?" I asked.

"If we do nothing the rains will wash away the road. Big stones and trees will fall on it. The elephant will tear up the bridges."

"What must be done?" I knew that this thing could not be ignored.

"We must call Ifarawala."

Ifarawala was not what I had expected at all. He was a fat, cheerful man full of laughter and bawdy stories and self-confidence. He was the village butcher. Exorcizing spirits was only a side-line I discovered, but he had built up quite a good practice.

He was very businesslike. Rather indecently so, I thought. We all expect a certain amount of pomp and mumbo-jumbo from our specialists but it only took Ifarawala ten minutes to exorcize our road. One or two marks on trees, a few simple spells and it was all over.

"It should be all right now," he said.

I didn't feel that he had done very much for the nine shillings we paid him. But the others seemed quite satisfied.

When I said good-bye to Old Man Abi I asked him why they hadn't told me about the country being haunted before.

He paused a little before he replied. He was a careful and deliberate man.

"Well," he said in the end, "we thought that if we told you at the beginning you would laugh at us. And then we couldn't have asked you afterwards.

"But," he went on, "by the time the road was finished so much had been done, so many difficulties overcome that part of you was in that road, and we felt that whether or not you really believed in the spirits that haunted this country, you wouldn't take the risk of not appeasing them."

I asked one more obvious question.

"It is true," he replied. "It is true that we could have called him afterwards without telling you, but, then"—he spread his hands—"but then who would have paid?"

CHAPTER THIRTY-TWO

The End of the Fly-Switch

A WEEK or so before I was due to leave for England reports started coming in that trouble was brewing in what I had always thought of as a particularly quiet and remote part of the District. It wasn't, I gathered, that they had a grievance against the Government over taxes or the price of ground-nuts or the lack of rain, as was usually the explanation. They were quarrelling over a piece of land. The men were busy sharpening their knives and spears, and the women were egging them on, as usual, with taunts and invidious comparisons about their virility in war and other irrelevant matters. I thought I had better go and see what was going on.

I took the messenger with the infinitely creased face with me, and my elderly cook. I piled them into the back of the car and we drove as far as the road went. After that, for about four hours, we walked. I left word at the village for them to send my camp-bed and a few other things on afterwards with porters. My cook refused to be parted from his cooking-pots so we left him behind too. He was a man of the coast and he viewed these up-country people with a mixture of extreme caution and deep suspicion which reminded me of the way the Cornish feel about people from Devon, and *vice versa*.

I hadn't sent word that I was coming but I expected that

somehow, by what people call the "bush-telegraph," they would have got to know. But the bush-telegraph is in fact just as uncertain as more modern methods of communication, and in this case they didn't seem to have heard anything at all. When we arrived the village was quiet and peaceful. There were no spears and no taunting women. If they had had warning they might at least, I thought, have put on some sort of a show, if only to make me feel that all my climbing and sweating up to their distant hills had been worth while. The people who lived there had very good manners.

My messenger however spat with disgust. "These people have no respect. Trouble? There isn't even a corpse!"

But the next morning when I met the people from the two villages which were quarrelling over their boundaries there was certainly plenty of tension. They had been told to leave their weapons behind and they did, but as if to compensate for this lack they had sharpened up their tongues. The men had been told to leave their womenfolk behind too, but we could see them gathered in colourful groups in the dark background of the trees. Bit by bit they edged their way forward and by the end of the morning they all had ringside seats.

The disputed area was a valley between two Chiefdoms that had been unoccupied and unused for as long as anyone could remember. Although many years ago the boundary had been agreed as a line between two hills, no one had ever troubled to work out the exact run of this line on the ground, for the very good reason that there was nothing worth bothering about in between. A few weeks before, however, one of the Chiefs had settled some pestering relations-by-concubinage in this area to keep them quiet and to occupy them a long way away from the place where he lived himself.

When this happened the other Chief became quite, quite

sure that the valley belonged to him. When I asked him why he had shown this sudden interest he said it was a matter of principle.

A dispute of this sort was not uncommon in this, as in other areas, but usually the Chiefs concerned settled it among themselves. In this case, however, the Chiefs were bitter enemies, and each for years had been looking for an excuse to get at the other's throat. This was just what they wanted, and neither they nor their people clearly had any intention of settling it amicably.

"Why are you so sure," I asked, "that this is your land?"

I spoke first to the elder of the two Chiefs. He was a useless drink-sodden old man, and I didn't like him very much.

"My grandmother . . ." he started:

". . . was the daughter of a goat." The other side completed the sentence for him.

"Tell your people to be quiet," I said to the other Chief. He was a rogue, but rather a likeable one. He had a horrible cast in one eye, but he was, I gathered, a great man for the girls.

"My grandmother," the old man continued, "used to pasture her pigs in this valley."

This piece of family history evoked squeals of laughter from the other side, and a few obvious grunts as well. I realized that I hadn't understood the finer nuances of this exchange, and I thought it better not to ask.

I also realized that this sort of thing could go on for hours. In any case I had come here to keep the peace, not to settle the dispute. One was often tempted when one was busy, or the weather was especially hot, to do the easier thing, and settle quarrels, and many other things oneself. But that wasn't what we were there for. Our job was not to rule but to help and, if need be, make them rule themselves. We wanted something that would last, so that when we left it could run by itself. Disputes between Chiefs were especially tricky, and because of that it was especially important to try and create some machinery of settlement which one hoped would stand the test of time.

I knew that these two particular Chiefs would never settle their quarrel on their own, and before I had left on this journey I had therefore had to lay on an alternative solution. There were nine Chiefs in the District altogether, and they met once a quarter as a Council of Chiefs to debate and decide matters affecting the whole area. Since the events described in "Election Day" they also had an advisory body of men elected by the people. This clearly was the sort of organization on which they would have to rely to settle disputes like this in the future, when there might be no British Commissioners to do it for them. The sooner they started, therefore, the better.

Communications were rather sketchy then, and it took some time to gather my team together and get them up into their remote hills. But by the evening they had all arrived. The next morning I went with them to the valley and left them to it.

"Where are you going?" they asked. The two outside Chiefs I had called on were excellent men and not unduly concerned at being asked to settle other people's problems, but the three elected men, a schoolmaster, a clerk and a trader, looked apprehensive and out of place in their town clothes in these bucolic hills.

"I am going to fish," I said. "I will be back in the evening."

About two hours' walk away, I knew, was a stream that one of my predecessors had stocked with trout. I had brought a rod with me, just in case.

As I was leaving one of the arbitrating Chiefs came up to

me. With him was the schoolmaster, a man who hid large reserves of eloquence and invective behind his quiet manner and shy smile.

"Bwana?" they asked.

"Yes," I said, "what is it?"

"May we borrow your fly-switch?"

"Yes," I said. "But why?"

They smiled, but they didn't say anything. I gave it to them.

"Good luck with the fish!" they called.

I only caught two trout, as far as I remember, and they were both rather small, but it was cool and pleasant and peaceful under the trees, and the tumbling stream and the mossy rocks were not unlike the upper reaches of a Devon stream. A small boy watched me, silently at first from the safety of the other bank and then, with less reticence, holding the net at my side, but otherwise I didn't see a soul. When later in the afternoon I left the river I did so with a small lump in my throat. I wondered whether I should ever see it or fish in it again.

As soon as I got back I knew that they had settled it. I could see it in their faces and sense it in the air. The fly-switch, I saw, was lying on the table by my bed.

"The solution was rather complicated," they said, and I knew that I was not expected to ask what exactly the solution was or how it had been achieved.

"They have accepted it," said the schoolmaster. And that was enough.

Soon afterwards I left for England, and it was some years before I went back to Africa. I left some of my belongings behind, but the Sultan's fly-switch went with me. I have it still, but the intricate pattern on the leather is worn and faded now and the gloss on the hair is dulled; and its day, I think, is done.